REAL
GARDENING

REAL GARDENING

STEPHEN LACEY

MICHAEL JOSEPH
an imprint of
PENGUIN BOOKS

MICHAEL JOSEPH

Published by the Penguin Group
Penguin Books Ltd, 80 Strand, London WC2R 0RL, England
Penguin Putnam Inc., 375 Hudson Street, New York, New York 10014, USA
Penguin Books Australia Ltd, Ringwood, Victoria, Australia
Penguin Books Canada Ltd, 10 Alcorn Avenue, Toronto, Ontario, Canada M4V 3B2
Penguin Books India (P) Ltd, 11 Community Centre, Panchsheel Park, New Delhi – 110 017, India
Penguin Books (NZ) Ltd, Cnr Rosedale and Airborne Roads, Albany, Auckland, New Zealand
Penguin Books (South Africa) (Pty) Ltd, 24 Sturdee Avenue, Rosebank 2196, South Africa

Penguin Books Ltd, Registered Offices: 80 Strand, London WC2R 0RL, England

www.penguin.com

First published 2002
1

Set in 11/16 pt Monotype Sabon
Typeset by Rowland Phototypesetting Ltd, Bury St Edmunds, Suffolk
Printed in England by Butler & Tanner Ltd, Frome and London

A CIP catalogue record for this book is available from the British Library

ISBN 0–718–14462–7

← Title page: Bluebells and *Brunnera macrophylla* seed between the green spikes of *Tellima grandiflora* Rubra Group in a shady corner of my garden in spring.

← Jacket photograph: A blaze of Californian poppy, *Eschscholzia californica*, at The Garden House, Devon. A hardy annual, it can be sown direct into the border in spring, and will self-sow thereafter, flowering for months.

To my wonderful Mother
Sarah, Robert and Julie

Emma Phillips and Tom Shaw
And to the memory of John Bird

NOTE

The following symbols are used for trees and shrubs in the plant lists:

- deciduous
- evergreen

CONTENTS

INTRODUCTION

Gardening has had me seriously hooked since my late teens. My job revolves around visiting gardens and meeting gardeners. At home, I dig and sow, plot and scheme. But even on the London Underground last week, I caught myself thinking about mulberries.

This book is an exposé of my addiction, but also a sharing of experiences and ideas from home and abroad. It is a look at the process of garden-making, step by step, from inspiration to reality: getting started, choosing your plants, deciding how to put them together, and experimenting along the way.

Making a garden involves taking lots of decisions but this can be confusing, especially when confronted by all the juicy options (and horrors) now bombarding us via television, books and magazines. This is my way of charting a course. These are the plants I wouldn't be without, and the planting ideas that have me smitten.

For me, garden-making is slow-fuse, not quick-fix. Getting a feel for your plot and conjuring up the right mood takes time. The TV programmes suggest it can all be done in a weekend. But you know the saying: act in haste, repent at leisure. In any case, the process is half the fun.

← An encounter with plants and the natural world is, for me, the principal point of a garden. Here *Nectaroscordium siculum* subsp. *bulgaricum* poses as if butter wouldn't melt in its mouth; you will need to watch what its questing roots are up to. An intriguing May bulb, it wants well-drained soil in sun or part-shade.

BEING REALISTIC

Ideas can be gleaned from almost anywhere, but I have learned that it is wise to stay in tune with reality. There is absolutely no sense waltzing between the polished borders of an icon like Sissinghurst in a state of euphoria, only to come home, take one look at your own plot, and feel deeply depressed. You are never going to have a garden like Sissinghurst, so you may as well forget it.

Expertise apart, there are eight pairs of hands working on those borders, staking, dead-heading, interplanting with bulbs and wallflowers, then replacing the bulbs and wallflowers with summer annuals . . . To achieve that curtain of *Clematis* 'Perle d'Azur' across the wide, semi-circular wall requires someone to be up a ladder, tying in shoots, for weeks. It is the same with those pristine gardens that open to the public on Sunday afternoons for the National Gardens Scheme. They are somebody's full-time job.

I spent a good five years trying to make a Sissinghurst out of my own plot, but fifteen years on, there is no longer much trace of it. Home for me is a one-acre town garden on the North Wales border, dominated by a brick and tile house of the Edwardian Arts and Crafts period and enclosed by walls of varying heights. At one stage we were nicely treed-in, too, but then next door's plot was clear-felled for a housing development, forcing me to install my own tree defences against the new neighbours, which have still some way to go.

The Sissinghurst formula of hedged compartments, trim lawns, and finely orchestrated flower displays seemed to suit the site perfectly. Only slowly did I become aware of the maintenance burden I was piling on, made more hopeless by the fact that I was spending more than half the year in London or on the road. Much as I loved the work, there were too many fiddly borders to get around in the time available.

I could manage one or two impressive weeks, around the end of May, after the winter and spring tidy-up was finally over and before the tide of growth became too great to stem. I even opened for the National Gardens Scheme. But then the gates were slammed shut, and somehow I had to parry all further

→ At home, the Edwardian design of rectangles and circles provides the framework for a series of seasonal borders, in which I am practising increasingly freestyle planting. I remain addicted to clipped box and pots of tulips.

requests to see it. My university tutor used to cite a 'middle ear infection' whenever he couldn't face hearing one of my hastily written French essays; this became a favourite excuse of mine, too – plausible, recurring, but not life-threatening.

RELAXING YOUR GRIP

But the more I travelled, the more I began to appreciate that there were other ways of gardening. One May, I went with friends to Kerdalo, a wooded garden that filled an entire combe on the remote Brittany coast. It was the work of a Russian artist, Prince Peter Wolkonsky, and an adventurous undertaking since he didn't begin it until he was sixty-five – an age when many people are thinking of moving into town, to be close to the hospital. But here he was, still busy at the age of ninety-six, planting tree magnolias which weren't going to bloom for fifteen years, and making a fountain in his studio out of wire and resin. (Sadly, he died two years later.)

All his plants were carefully placed (scented white *Rhododendron* 'Lady Alice Fitzwilliam' by the back door 'to counter the odours of the kitchen') and beautifully colour-schemed: blended banks of pink and white azaleas and purple-leaved Japanese maples; spiky yellow asphodel in front of a cloud of blue ceanothus; a wall of tender scarlet lobster claw (*Clianthus*) above the white stars of Mexican orange blossom (*Choisya*).

But, even around the house, the scenes weren't in the least manicured. Daisies speckled the rough-edged lawns; bluebells seemed to infiltrate every flower-bed; hart's-tongue ferns, together with the pink and white Mexican daisy, *Erigeron karvinskianus*, bobbed along the paving cracks; wisteria had leapt its pergola to scramble up a tree; and perennials, such as yellow-cylindered *Euphorbia characias* subsp. *wulfenii*, were allowed to drop a few seedlings, colonize, and generally make themselves at home.

There was no attempt at all at an immaculate horticultural showcase. Instead of itsy-bitsy, high-maintenance flower-beds, a few good plants were allowed to take control in each area. Wildflowers were welcomed in. At home, unless I kept everything smart, my Sissinghurst-style efforts just looked dishevelled and chaotic. But at Kerdalo, a partnership seemed to have been struck with nature. Indeed, in many parts of the garden it was like taking a walk through a fantasy countryside. And on a country walk, you don't think, 'Oh dear, how messy,' you accept the natural ebb and flow without blinking. So you did here. It just fuelled the atmosphere of enchantment.

TAKING YOUR CUE FROM NATURE

Beth Chatto's garden, at Elmstead Market near Colchester, was another eye-opener. By contrast, this is a serious showcase flower garden, but one that follows very few of the traditional design principles. There are no straight lines, no internal hedges, no box edgings or topiary shapes, and no banked-up, staked flower displays. Lawns and paths meander about in sinuous curves. The entire structure of the garden – the divisions of space, the focal points, the

← *Euphorbia characias* subsp. *wulfenii* seeds itself among forget-me-nots on my sunny terrace. But its milky sap is a hazard: it once had me in Casualty.

backbones of the beds – comes from the natural forms of plants, from weeping willows and rocket-shaped swamp cypresses to cushions of sedums and round-leaved bergenias. It is a garden very much built around foliage patterns.

Part of the excitement for me was seeing how the traditional cast of perennials – the high-maintenance dahlias, delphiniums and the like – were replaced by simpler, subtler, wilder sorts of plant, that stood up by themselves and needed very little cosseting. Many of these plants – the wispy grasses, the thistles, the cow parsleys – Edwardian gardeners would have dismissed as weeds. But tastes were changing, their beauty was obvious, and Beth Chatto was leading the way. And in the process, I was realizing that it wasn't just flowers, but every aspect of a plant's growth, from stem to seedhead, that was a potential star turn.

The other important lesson was seeing, so clearly demonstrated, that a garden is really a collection of habitats, almost exactly corresponding to what is available to plants in the wild. A shady garden is like a wood, part-shade is like a woodland glade; an open, sunny flower-bed is like a meadow; poor, dry soil is what you find around the Mediterranean; rich, moist soil is what you get in the American prairies.

Sure, you can fight your conditions, by irrigating, changing the soil, or pumping in the fertilizer. But the Chatto message is that if instead you work with it – match each habitat to the right cast of plants, in other words those found growing in that same habitat in nature – you make life much easier for yourself. And following this principle, Beth has turned her own unpromising site – previously designated unfit for farming, with a very low average rainfall (hardly any in a typical summer), and soil ranging from dust to waterlogged clay – into some of the finest woodland gardens, gravel gardens and moist meadow gardens you will ever meet.

Today, almost everywhere I go, from Kensington to Indianapolis, I find gardeners experimenting with a more nature-inspired style of planting. Once, the traditional English country house ideal was carried all over the globe, terraced lawns and rose-beds merrily stamped on any landscape as far away as Australia, so that wherever you went, you must have got a sense of *déjà vu*. But today, people are starting to enjoy their regional quirks of location, climate, geology and vegetation.

A Californian garden is more likely to be sculpted in gravel and cacti; a New Zealand garden in grasses and tree ferns (formerly thought good enough only to make fences) – though I did sympathize with the inhabitants of Rotorua, whose soil is actively volcanic, steam rising between their plants (the consolation, I was told, is that you can lower your evening meal into the herbaceous border, and have it slow-cooked for when you get home).

In the same way, the new taste for British wildflowers is beginning to give our own gardens a stronger sense of their locality, drawing in wildlife in the process. The results can have a deep emotional impact. I have heard several stories of elderly visitors coming to gardens with recreated meadows of scarlet poppies, blue cornflowers and yellow corn marigolds, alive with bees and butterflies, and their eyes filling with tears. Suddenly, they were reconnected with their childhood, with a lost countryside.

In Holland, gardeners like Ton ter Linden and Piet Oudolf have been perfecting a naturalistic version of the traditional herbaceous border, formal in design but weaving together grasses, wildflowers and plants with long-lasting seedheads. Piet Oudolf's borders tend to be tall and muscular, with the plants grown in architectural clumps; Ton ter Linden's were (he has since sold up and moved) flowing, jewel-like and dreamy, richly coloured but employing a limited range of plants, repeated again and again in meadowy rhythms.

In France, designers Eric Ossart, André Maurières and Louis Benech have been loosening up traditional summer bedding by creating kaleidoscopes that mix showy and simple plants, annuals and perennials – white cosmos and red salvias in a haze of hairy *Pennisetum* grasses, for example – again inspired by the mingled patterns of wild meadows.

Back in Britain, such ideas are being taken on in leaps and bounds by the unstoppable Keith Wiley, head gardener at The Garden House, Buckland Monachorum, on the edge of Dartmoor in Devon. From the old walled garden, developed by Lionel Fortescue until his death in 1981, Keith has expanded into

almost ten acres of field beyond, creating heath gardens, alpine gardens, woodland glades, water gardens, prairie gardens, Cretan meadows, South African meadows, and in the time it has taken me to write this paragraph probably a few more besides, all prompted by images of, and visits to, flower-rich landscapes around the world.

He doesn't try to reproduce them exactly, but lets his imagination rip, interpreting them with whatever plants he thinks will give the most spectacular results. It has become one of my favourite gardens, and many photos of it appear in this book.

↑ | This vibrant scene of annuals and tender perennials at The Garden House was inspired by the flowering of the South African veld. To resemble conditions in the wild, the beds have been topped with a layer of gritty sand, with compost beneath.

Perhaps the most radical new experiments are being conducted in Germany, for here much of the conventional wisdom on the cultivation of plants is being turned on its head. Traditionally, we have been taught to prepare and maintain a rich and hearty soil for our plants, particularly our perennials, with regular dressings of manure and fertilizer. The paradox spotted by the Germans is that, in the wild, most of our garden plants actually grow on quite poor soils.

What happens in gardens, when you inject them with all this nitrogen, is that they tend to become excessively vigorous, tall and leafy. In turn, this means they need regular lifting, staking, dividing and summer-watering to perform well. By cutting down the fertility – even to the extent of stripping off topsoil – and matching the right cast of plants to the right habitat, German designers like Rosemarie Weisse in Munich's Westpark and Urs Walser at Hermannshof in Weinheim have, sure enough, managed to build complex communities of trees, shrubs, grasses and perennials that behave very much as they would in the wild, requiring little more than periodic editing.

Here, one of the first gardeners to take this German research on board has been Judy Pearce at Lady Farm, in the village of Chelwood, west of Bath. Though not a keen gardener herself, she was encouraged by her garden designer friend Mary Payne to attend a symposium on German planting at Kew. Fired up by what they heard, they embarked almost immediately on their return home on the transformation of a small hillside into a sweeping panorama of grasses and perennials – burying Judy's husband's tennis court in the process.

Following German principles, they did no soil improvement but planted directly into the heavy clay – a stony, Mediterranean-type planting on the upper slopes, and a taller, denser, prairie scheme on the damper, lower slopes. Five years on it continues to look stunning, as the photos in this book prove, and, as predicted, it has so far needed little maintenance beyond occasional weeding. The prairie section is simply strimmed, in late winter: the herbaceous border that you mow. And, of course, Judy herself is now a convert, even to the extent of allowing her husband to keep only brown cows in the surrounding fields. Black and white ones jar with the plants.

→ Next page: Purple Joe Pye weed, *Eupatorium purpureum* 'Atropurpureum', and the erect grass *Calamagrostis* × *acutiflora* 'Karl Foerster' create a prairie rhythm at Lady Farm, Somerset.

So, in response to all this stimulation, my own approach to gardening has changed. I run the garden differently, and I plan most of my borders differently. On the other hand, I couldn't be classed as one of the 'new

naturalists' I have mentioned above, because I am still as addicted to clipped box shapes and old French roses, tripods of sweet peas and cauldrons of Dutch tulips, as I am to corncockles and giant oat grass. But you don't have to choose between the old and the new, the formal and the wild. They can work beautifully together. It is all a matter of finding a look that you love, and a composition that doesn't break your back.

1 — THE BIG IDEA

'Every garden should tell a single story.' I remember reading this line in a book by the French designer Gilles Clément. Walking around my own garden, it sometimes feels as if there are as many stories as in the *Arabian Nights*. But he is right. Somehow, the elements in every scene have to knit together, and not look like an assortment of impulse buys from the reclamation yard and garden centre (even if they are). And, more than that, these scenes need to connect, so your garden appears all of a piece.

Where to begin? Well, no one starts with a completely bare plot. At the very least there is a house in it, and probably the odd tree and mature shrub besides. Then you have got a particular soil, climate, aspect, and lie of land. Beyond the garden wall are further influences, whether country fields, factory chimneys, or simply the trees and shrubs that the neighbours are growing. All these are contributing to what designers call 'a sense of place', and pointing you in certain directions.

SOMEWHERE OVER THE RAINBOW

On the other hand, gardens should be a little larger than life, don't you think? You want moments of fantasy that send you into another orbit. Sadly, we can't all manage a fairytale tower (like Sissinghurst), a ruined monastery (like The Garden House), or even a striped tent in the meadow (like Tom Stuart-Smith), but a few dreamy objects – spider's-web benches and soaring obelisks, in my case – or spots of swashbucklingly unlikely planting can be enough.

← Previous page: On this narrow rectangular slope at The Garden House, Keith Wiley has taken one bold idea and carried it through with conviction and panache: the recipe for all successful garden design.

As the TV makeover gardeners show us, you can go further still, painting your entire garden Moroccan blue and lipstick pink, and packing in the palm trees. Such Disneyworld scenes get you thinking, even if, as they do me, the results also make you feel a bit queasy.

Nick and Pam Coote's enclosed Oxford garden is easier on the eye, but no less magical. Stepping through the gate is like passing through the cupboard into Narnia. Suddenly, England is exchanged for the Riviera. Painted shutters on the house windows and a parasol on the terrace strike the mood, and off you saunter, along walks lined with palms and blue African agapanthus, past beds of scarlet pelargoniums set into emerald, irrigated lawn, and into glades of hydrangeas and lilies.

The spell is broken only when you go behind the scenes and see the mind-boggling greenhouse back-up and pot-lugging machinery needed to support exotic plant life in this bone-chilling city (brrr, I remember those student winters in front of a single-bar electric heater).

In big cities, escapism can help keep you sane. So, in London, where I have an 8ft/2.5m square first-floor terrace, I have taken the plunge, too. In tiny spaces like this, the principal point of a garden is to be an extra room, which

↑ Such apparitions – here between hedges and shrub roses in Tom Stuart-Smith's Hertfordshire garden – nicely loosen your grip on reality.

you can spill into on warm days. With the help of a friend, Gareth Hughes, I have turned mine into a dining-room on the theme of a Venetian pontoon, with a decking floor and side-screens of yacht canvas, strung between striped and gilded mooring-posts. It is a fine antidote to the glum, grey surroundings, and hides me away from the twitching net curtains.

Because I am absent a lot, I keep the planting simple. I grow only loquats, *Eriobotrya japonica*, installed in terracotta pots and pruned as standards. This large-leaved evergreen (from the Far East, but cultivated all around the Mediterranean for centuries) has proved extremely forgiving, allowing me to abandon it, without water, for periods of up to a fortnight during the summer; the leaves droop, but soon bounce back. Apart from its exotic foliage, it provides vanilla-scented white flowers in early spring, and, given a bit of sun, yellow fruits later. These are juicy and sweet, but completely tasteless. Still, quite impressive to be able to harvest dessert at dinner, 15ft/4.5m above the street.

EAST MEETS WEST

Japanese gardens were a popular fantasy in the 1970s, but I should be wary of reproducing them lock, stock and deer-scarer. All that symbolism and raked sand is so alien to our Western labrador-friendly traditions, more oddity than enchantment. I'm afraid I chuckled in the Huntington Botanic Garden in Los Angeles, watching a couple consulting their map as they looked down on a reproduction of the classic oriental scene, complete with pagoda and maples. 'Do you think this is the Japanese garden or the Shakespeare garden?' asked the man.

On the other hand, take some of the ideas – the simplicity, the delight in

↑ One of the largest-leaved garden evergreens, the loquat is hardy in London and coastal areas, but needs protection elsewhere.

plant shape, the beauty of weathered rock – and set them in a home context, and the results certainly can float you away. The best small front garden I have ever seen is at Carol Valentine's garden, in Montecito just north of LA, where designer Isabelle Greene has pursued a minimalist style she calls California Zen.

It is a rectangular plot, enclosed by 7ft/2.25m creamy stucco walls and laid to gravel. At either end are trees, native oaks at one, and at the other *Maytenus boaria*, a small evergreen Chilean tree, in appearance something like a slim weeping willow (rare here, but hardy and well worth hunting down). The focal point, under the dappled canopy of the oaks, is nothing more than a vertical column of local rock, silhouetted against the stucco, and in front of it a narrow irregular pond, edged in rough slates which randomly spill outwards as islands in the gravel.

Their nimbus pattern echoes the gappy habit of the trees, and this theme of broken shapes is then picked up by the water and pondside planting, which comprises open, angular aquatics like water hawthorn (*Aponogeton*), together with filigree ferns, and cyperus and papyrus sedges, which carry their needle-like leaves in bunches, at different heights, and above tall, bare stems. One simple planting idea carried through with conviction: quite brilliant.

FORM FROM FUNCTION

At the outset you have to decide what you most want from your garden, and I am assuming that, like me, your answer will be, first and foremost, an encounter with the natural world – to get to know plants, to watch wildlife, and to follow the changing seasons. But gardens are also for living in, and, at the very least, we all need a sitting-out area and all-weather access.

In city gardens, these can take up most of the available space. Many people, therefore, wisely decide to go the whole hog and treat their plots as courtyard rooms. The paving becomes the carpet, maybe even echoing a pattern inside the house (say, by running lines of red brick between expanses of grey flagstone); any small lawn becomes like a rug; the table becomes the inviting centrepiece of the room; and there might even be pictures on the walls. One garden I visited in Washington DC had a wall mosaic by Chagall – probably worth more than the house.

But, as in a conservatory, this can still be a green, sensuous environment. As a focal point there might be the sight and sound of water, whether falling from wall spout into basin (tricky to get the noise right, though, so it doesn't have everyone running to the loo), or as a sheet-waterfall down pebbles. And then there are the plants. Most appealing may be those with sculptural, year-round leaf qualities, but I wouldn't overdo it, or your planting will look very static and contrived. Mix in some of the simpler flowers and leaves, too, and make sure there is plenty of scent and finger-enticing texture.

In larger gardens, the areas needed for outdoor living can be absorbed into a bigger picture, allowing the garden to feel more obviously in the grip of nature. But making practical decisions about how you are going to use your plot is still a good starting point for a design.

Obviously, the area immediately next to the house is the handiest for eating and entertaining. But it will not necessarily be the most scenic or sunny. A local octogenarian, Mrs Lawton, universally known as Auntie May, had her sitting area (sensibly roofed against the elements) at the very end of her garden, which meant at the top of a very long, steep slope. Each day she carried her breakfast up there, and then spent the rest of the morning getting back down, gardening

on the way. 'I specialize in one thing,' she told me. 'Seats.' There was one at each level, for wherever the sun might be. Slopes were ideal for the elderly, she asserted, because to get at the weeds, you only had to bend half as far.

The more seductive areas of a garden soon impress themselves on you, and help you deconstruct your plot. Yes, I think that is where I shall put the barbecue . . . grow my herbs . . . have my perennial border . . . park the baby . . . Then, it is a matter of deciding how your chosen elements will be strung together.

A few words about borders. The best vantage point is invariably down their length, not at right angles – when you can see all the gaps. And make them as deep and generous as possible, so there is scope for backing shrubs and layers of perennials. Narrow beds are hard to plant well. A slight incline in soil level, higher at the back, is also a good idea where plants are to be of a similar height.

STRAIGHT LINES AND NATURAL CURVES

Garden style is generally discussed in terms of formal or informal. But rigid formality is deadly dull (French parks) and complete informality is chaos. The most appealing garden designs are a marriage between the two, the most potent garden images invariably those that combine, and contrast, manmade with natural forms, straight lines with curves.

Around the house, I like the scales to be tipped in favour of the formal, to help anchor the house in the garden, and to suggest someone is at the helm. Interlocking squares and rectangles of flagstone, lawn and water, hedges, topiary shapes and blocks of evergreen shrubs – that sort of thing. Architectural and geometric.

In a traditional design, these would be pieced together in symmetry, leading the eye in straight lines. But it is often more rewarding to go for an abstract composition, which takes eyes and feet on a less obvious route. Instead of offering mirror images, you balance different shapes, masses and voids

← | Asymmetry, clean lines and abstract shapes give a contemporary feel to the sitting area outside Tom Stuart-Smith's converted barn. Soft colours keep the mood relaxed.

asymmetrically, as you do when furnishing a sitting-room. (Asymmetry is a bit more complicated to get right, so you will almost certainly need to play about on graph paper.)

The visual excitement then comes from inserting free-form plants among the hard lines – perennials spilling over paving, say, or a tree erupting behind the flat planes of a hedge. In this role, the snakebark maple (*Acer capillipes*) I planted beside the holly hedge at home has turned out to be a huge hit. I knew the white and green veins of the trunk and branches would stand out brightly against the dark hedge, but I had no inkling of the impact our movement-activated security lamp would have. On winter evenings, the light converts the tree's dull red twigs into a blaze of scarlet coral. All it takes for the show is a wave of the hand.

You can use this formula of informal planting inside a formal groundplan for the whole garden, and in a walled town plot that might make sense. The

↑ Chunky strips of stone paving and flanking buttresses of yew provide a strong, permanent frame to the view from Tom's barn, along borders of salvias, geraniums and white lychnis.

→ The white tiers of *Cornus controversa* 'Variegata', in combination with evergreens, gives my front door its year-round furnishing. The plum-coloured twigs look good in winter, especially when the security light is activated.

border planting might become more mingled and relaxed as you ventured further from the house, but the strong lines of paths, lawns and hedges would maintain a civilized order.

Alternatively, as the garden recedes from the house, you can allow the formality gradually to dissolve into meandering paths, freestyle expanses of grass and water, and curvaceous flower-beds, so there is a sense of progression into the countryside, whether real or not. Here, the design highlights will come from introducing manmade forms – a seat, a gate, or the arch of a bridge – into the sea of plants. These will become your focal points, helping to structure the scenes and make them more welcoming.

BONDING HOUSE AND GARDEN

The house is the largest object in your garden, and shouldn't look stranded. It needs to be linked visually with the garden. Terraces, patios and pergolas extend building lines into the garden; climbing plants, and flanking groups of trees and shrubs, bring the garden to the house.

If the house is old, it is nice to have a historical echo of it in the garden. Not

a wall-to-wall reproduction, but perhaps an ornament, a paint colour, or a tree evocative of that period. A rummage through National Trust gardens can put you in the picture.

On the Cotswold escarpment near Stroud, John and Fiona Owen have cleverly taken the Gothic detailing from the window of their converted chapel and reproduced it around the garden in seats, summerhouse and bird-table. Their gates, pergola and rose supports are also in the shape of a Gothic arch. The garden itself is freestyle and cottagey, on many different levels up the hillside, but these elements are enough to unify it and give it an unmistakable identity.

Using a similar colour and type of building material forms an obvious bond between house and garden, whether stone, gravel or brick. In any event, I like my materials mellow and natural (my local orange brick is a disaster, not losing its glare even after 100 years). Wood I am using more and more. I am a fan of pressure-treated decking, especially in combination with water – protruding over a pond, or acting as a boardwalk through reeds and bog plants. Old railway sleepers are splendid as risers to gravel steps, as well as for retaining walls. My shady paths are dressed in chipped bark. And my fences are now all woven willow and hazel panels – though it is painful having to replace them every five to ten years.

Glass is too attention-grabbing for me; even my greenhouse annoys me, especially when flashing in the sun (I noticed that someone in Atlanta had disguised his by fitting trellis to the gable end, which I thought was a classy solution). As for expanses of square ceramic tiles, they make me think of public lavatories.

THE HEART OF A GARDEN

The heart of a garden is going to be its principal open space, and this wants to be as generously proportioned as you can make it. This was my big mistake in Oxford: more than three people on the central circle of lawn and it felt a crush.

And to make the heart of the garden inviting, and to encourage you to linger, there needs to be something really engaging there, year round. Perhaps it will be a nice view back to the house, or out into the countryside; a piece of architectural ornament or a characterful tree. But there is one feature that everyone can build a garden around, and that is water.

Water is the strongest magnet of all. Adults, children, wildlife, all gravitate to it. So it makes sense to give it prominence in the design, and put it where you want people to congregate. My own pool, just outside the kitchen window, is ideal for watching the comings and goings of the redwings, bramblings and goldfinches, but I wish I had centred the sitting areas and lawns around it, and made it the visual as well as the active hub.

Whether a formal rectangle, edged in stone or mown grass, or naturally curved and fringed in reeds, I like my ponds simple and tranquil. No fancy flowers or variegated leaves; certainly, no peeing cherubs. A raft of sulphur waterlilies, perhaps, or a belt of blue irises, but otherwise just the quiet pleasures of green vegetation, darting dragonflies and reflections. And bear in mind what is going to be reflected: infuriatingly, my own pond catches the corner of the garage extension.

In America, a black vegetable dye is sometimes added to the water to intensify the reflections. I have seen it used here only once, in Anthony Archer-Wills's former Sussex garden, where the pools are designed like crater lakes, connected by streams that run along cracks in the paving, as if following a geological fault line. Wonderfully mysterious. The dye is inert, and supposedly harmless to wildlife including fish, though I imagine they must bump into things a bit.

JOURNEYS AND DESTINATIONS

In larger gardens, there may be a string of open spaces leading up to, or away from, the principal space, each with its own secondary theme. But again, it is good to have one Big Idea connecting them. The hub of Elizabeth Woodhouse's Sussex garden is the brick terrace adjacent to her house, from which circular tiers of brick steps descend to a spacious lawn. This is also in the shape of a circle, with a round copper cauldron as its centrepiece. From here, the eye is channelled between vertical Irish yews into a second circle of lawn, and then, through a further narrow opening, out on to the hillside field beyond. A box topiary, clipped as a wagon wheel, adds a further circle off to the side. Each area of garden has its own distinct plantings and colour schemes, but the circles give the composition a clear unity.

This is an example of the formal way of linking spaces, progressing from one to the other along a central axis. But circles make it feel less rigid, and the contraction and expansion, from wide lawn to narrow opening to wide lawn, makes the journey more interesting.

A meandering axis line, and a concealed destination, whets the appetite for exploration still more. This is one of the charms of Denmans, John Brookes's garden near Chichester. The terrace is a self-contained scene, focused on a group of silver birches raised up on contoured ground, but beyond, winding gravel paths half-hidden by trees and shrubs suggest that there is more to see. So off you set into the shadows. The paths soon open out on to lawn, spliced by a curving gravel 'river'. The same curves appear in the grass, for John has two heights of cut, short sward along the 'river' and meadow-length a couple

of feet back, which unite to create a powerful swirling momentum, and this propels you along to the end of the garden, where the reward is a lung of clear water, bordered by gravel 'beach'.

The eye is naturally drawn first to bright colours and then to strong shapes, and using these, you can direct the way that a design is perceived and explored. A white-trunked birch, pale obelisk, or church spire on or beyond your boundary will emphasize distance and draw the surrounding landscape into the garden. The scene may be broad and floating, over waves of flowers or rippling contours, or it may be formalized by an avenue of trees or a procession of Irish yews.

The most ingenious eyecatcher I have come across belonged to the late David Hicks. He had installed a wooden pyramid in the field outside his Oxfordshire garden, but set on wheels. This was 'to foil the planners'. They couldn't very well prosecute, because it was technically a vehicle, and always moving. I was also taken with his moated writing pavilion, which had an electric drawbridge, hoisted when he didn't want to be disturbed. Both were part of a series of architectural ornaments which, with the box parterres, avenues and pleached tree enclosures, gave his garden a crisp, classical air.

Put a bold object in the foreground, and you stop the eye in its tracks and encourage foreground scrutiny. I exploit this at home with the aid of seats, pots, and even simple wooden tripods, which direct you to places where things are going on – an August flush of hardy cyclamen, maybe, or ripening grapes on the purple-leaved vine. Like David Hicks's pyramid, most of my objects are movable, and interchangeable. In small gardens, particularly, you can ring dramatic seasonal changes by having a store of different glazed pots and furniture up your sleeve, in the shed or garage, which you can pull out to contrast with different flower colours and events whenever you feel like it. I prefer my objects in plain colours and in simple organic or geometric shapes, so they complement but don't compete with the plants.

Too many eyecatchers are confusing, of course (as at Highgrove), but a judicious combination of foreground and more distant objects creates

← This view at Haseley Court, Oxfordshire, causes a double-take. The statue, set into a free-standing cube of box, is across the yard beyond.

perspective, and gives a series of punctuation points by which the eye can read the design. These can be in alignment, as in the walled garden within Denmans, where at intervals a stone ball, a terracotta urn, a clipped globe of variegated box and a blue Lutyens seat lead you along the path, each half-concealed from the other by billowing shrubs like ceanothus, euphorbia and purple berberis.

Or the eyecatchers can be on a zig-zag, leading the eye from one side of the garden to the other, and so fully exploiting its width. I know a small garden in Chelsea structured like this, with a bold phormium in the left foreground, a dazzling white-splashed euonymus middle-distance right, and a pale-trunked snakebark maple in the left corner of the back wall. The effect is to divide the space into abstract triangles. Beth Chatto plans many of her views in a similar way, often with rocket-shaped conifers as the eyecatchers marking the corners. These are buttressed to the ground with tiers of shrubs and perennials, and in the open space between there will be low eyecatchers, like an eruption of giant gunnera, a potted agave, or the white façade of her bungalow, to lure you on.

A garden should have you guessing, and keep you entertained. Open gates are irresistible; views partly blocked by planting or trellis have to be investigated. Having to duck under a branch, squeeze between shrubs, or navigate stepping stones over a stream just adds to the adventure. And you must have ambushes – a monstrous lily, say, an overscaled statue, or a gash of red Goliath poppies – to stop you dead. They don't have to be sweet. Taking the ghost walk at Gunby Hall, Lincolnshire, in the twilight, you brush past cobwebby white perennials and stumble into junipers, kept to man height and width, which sway threateningly in the wind.

PLANTING THEMES

The mood of a garden, however, is invariably set by plants. And the way to make that mood strong is to have a coherent theme running through the planting. Traditionally, plants are themed almost entirely by colour, height and shape. The resulting borders may have nothing to do with nature. Indeed, they

often merrily partner plants from quite opposite ends of the ecological spectrum – a fat green hosta next to a lacy silver artemisia, say, or a Japanese maple beside a Mexican agave. It doesn't matter. They make a pretty picture and the eye can read it.

But it is ornamental planting with a more naturalistic feel, a freer spirit, and a more ecological basis that is at the heart of this book, bringing together plants which are all found in a similar type of habitat in the wild, and so have characteristics in common. Wild nature is hugely atmospheric, and the idea is to capture some of it in the garden. A garden might, therefore, be planted to give the flavour of woodland or meadow, jungle, heath, shingle beach, reedy marsh, Mediterranean hillside, Australian billabong . . . The possibilities are enormous.

But nature is there to offer guidelines, not as a straitjacket. Most plants are surprisingly adaptable, especially when a gardener is present to edit out the

↑ A combination of grasses, self-seeding verbena and casually repeated clumps of simple flowers like *Campanula lactiflora* gives a wild feel to this corner of The Garden House. Exploration is irresistible.

competition. So, if the look is right, and the plant doesn't mind, you can take a liberal view. Indeed, occasionally it pays dividends to break the rules completely – for instance, giving an aggressive plant exactly the opposite habitat to what it would prefer in order to restrain its vigour.

Traditional and naturalistic approaches can also be blended. High horticulture can be structured to look naturalistic (scarlet *Dahlia* 'Bishop of Llandaff' set among hazy purple *Verbena bonariensis*, as at Lady Farm); and naturalistic planting can be colour-coordinated to look painterly (white and cream erythroniums set among unfurling bronze *Polystichum* ferns, as at Knightshayes, Devon).

What's more, a garden can progress from one style to the other, perhaps by having more contrived and theatrical plantings near the house and more nature-inspired plantings further away. As you get to your boundaries, the planting may even turn purely native.

CREATING THE MOOD

How do you decide what planting theme to take up? Well, there may already be a mood to tap into, even in urban gardens. Trees are often a starting point for me.

An old apple and lilac, for instance, will invariably send me on an orchard tack, as they did in my narrow strip of a back garden when I lived near the centre of Oxford. The house was part of a low-rise Victorian brick and wattle-and-daub terrace, and there were many other lilacs and fruit trees in our row. If I hadn't inherited an apple tree, I would certainly have planted one, to stoke up the flavour of the neighbourhood.

I thought the place cried out for swags of climbing roses, self-seeding columbines, and jugs of foaming ale. But for the roses, the soil, exhausted to dust, needed a major boost, and I had five tons of horse manure deposited on the main road (my own Dreaming Spire), which I wheelbarrowed down the little passageway round to the back.

→ A cauldron of silver *Astelia chathamica* is the centrepiece of my orchard garden. As the apple trees and roses have expanded, I am now having to replace their sun-loving companion plants with shade-tolerant woodlanders.

Then, in went the jumble of cottage perennials and roses, structured by cones of box, and a few fast-growing shrubs like buddleia and pink-saucered *Lavatera* 'Barnsley'. In fact, this last made such an impact in such a short space of time (well set off by next door's purple-leaved plum) that I was surprised at my desk one afternoon by a passing wedding party of complete strangers who asked to have their photos taken in front of it.

Other town gardens feel more like glades in a wood. When I came to my plot in Wales, I found it fringed in tall trees, predominantly common lime and wild cherry, with an understorey of hollies. The woodland mood was obvious, and I was happy with this as my Big Idea. So I bolstered the boundaries with more trees and shrubs in sympathy with those already there, including small-leaved lime (*Tilia cordata*), a more handsome cousin of common lime, with a powerful flower scent; and Portugal laurel (*Prunus lusitanica*), a quick-growing counterpart to holly, which is my favourite screening plant bar none.

To echo all this in the borders, I installed different varieties of holly, and other dense, dark evergreens (osmanthus, viburnum, skimmia), together with amelanchier, which has similar blossom and leaf tints to wild cherry, but at a lower height. And to make the internal divisions within the garden, I planted other small trees evocative of woodland, such as maples, magnolias and Asian rowans. So that now, although there are a dozen distinct areas within it — water

garden, orchard garden, and all sorts of seasonal borders – the garden as a whole does have a certain unity (in the right light, anyway).

In Central London, the ubiquitous plane trees often convey quite a Mediterranean mood, which the mild winters and dry summers can help you foster. My friends Jonathan and Gillie Shaw are planning a formal Italian garden in their rectangular strip, designed as two terraced lawns, with a basin of water and flanking flights of steps as the central dividing feature. Slim Italian cypresses, and shade-tolerant box and bay trees, clipped as domes, are likely contenders for the borders. And so are olives, though even on a sunny London wall you are lucky to harvest enough fruits for a round of dry martinis.

STARTING OFF WITH A TREE

If there aren't any attractive trees in sight, then you can kick-start your garden by planting one yourself. It should be something with real charisma. I have just suggested a medlar, *Mespilus germanica*, to friends in South London, whose 60ft/18m garden backs on to a miserably dreary copse of misshapen sycamores (protected by Tree Preservation Orders, of course). They wanted a small tree that had a sense of history about it, but one that felt more rural than metropolitan. There was no contest: white flowers, splendid autumn colour, a pleasant bark and winter outline, and bizarre fruit, whose rude literary associations ought to plug a few gaps in dinner-party chatter.

On my north boundary at home, which is cut off from the rest of the garden by the house, I faced a different scene. My neighbours' trees were the proverbial riot of flower and leaf colour (cherries, magnolias, golden robinias, purple plums . . .) that desperately needed calming. The lynchpin seemed to be the Joneses' Scots pine tree. So, taking that as my theme, I planted three more pines along my narrow border. Then I was rather devious. I also presented one to each of my neighbours. (I am surprised more people don't think of giving as presents plants they would like to see in their view, but don't have room for themselves.)

Now there is a handsome stand of pines rising up, which will eventually dominate the scene; a more natural, landscape scale of planting will be struck; and a mood is being conjured up, which, with the help of euphorbias and cistus, I am now giving a Mediterranean slant.

COTTAGE GARDENS AND MEADOW BORDERS

On the other hand, an absence of trees can also suggest an approach. Maybe you have views of rolling farmland, or simply want to preserve your plot's open, sunny disposition. Here, instead of orchards and woods, your inspiration can come from meadows, coastline and rocky hillsides, where the dominant vegetation is of grasses and perennials, lightly or heavily peppered with sun-

↑ As a specimen tree, the medlar takes some beating.

loving shrubs, and with just the odd, widely spaced oak, rowan or pine on the skyline.

The cottage style is one option. This bucolic sort of garden, with its frothing flower borders inside neat hedged compartments, is really a scaled-down, artful version of the meadows and hedgerows around it, which is why it sits so well in the rural landscape. Trees are not an integral part of the style. Indeed, growing any tree other than a productive apple or damson would traditionally have been considered quite eccentric. 'There is one place for a tree, and that is in a wood,' as an old cottage gardener put it to me. Shade and thirsty roots were as welcome in his garden as they were over the hedge, in the farmer's cereal crop.

A straightforward design of squares and rectangles, overflowing with plants, is the cottage recipe. The principal structural elements are the hedges, paths, fences and walls, strengthened perhaps with some internal topiary. 'Puddings' is how the great cottage gardener Margery Fish described the wide-waisted clipped shapes that flanked the central pathway through her garden at East Lambrook, in the cider orchard countryside of Somerset, and gave it its backbone. They were formed of 'Fletcheri' cypresses, an odd choice – yew would have been more amenable to shaping and repairing.

Against these year-round features, the seasonal tides of snowdrops and pulmonarias, primroses and violets, daffodils and wallflowers, bluebells and columbines, hardy geraniums and delphiniums, phloxes and Japanese anemones, Michaelmas daisies and chrysanthemums, ebb and flow. Traditional shrubby ingredients would be roses and winter jasmine to plaster the walls, and a mock orange bush (*Philadelphus*) to mask the scent of the outdoor privy.

For a more natural interpretation of the meadowy look, you can sidestep the fancier plants, loosen up the clumpy planting, and weave in the grasses. In a country garden, such meadowy borders will simply melt into their surroundings, the grass shapes and green-to-parchment tints echoing what is happening over the fence. But they can bring a breath of country air into cities, too, as in Gareth Hughes's tiny terraced Richmond cottage, where the windows are half-hidden in a blur of flowering fennel and Stipa grass, enlivened by jewel-like specks of colour from poppies, purple verbena and much else. The beds are hardly more than 16 square feet, but they whisk you far from London.

The grass theme does not have to mean mingled and 'messy'. On the east coast of America, the design team of James van Sweden and Wolfgang Oehme have perfected a highly sculptural style by using big, single-species drifts of flowering grasses, and playing them against equally generous sweeps of perennials, water, terrace and decking. The planting design is strong enough not to have to rely on hedges and clipped evergreens for its structure, and looks as good contrasting with the white Federal offices of Washington DC as on the open shores of Chesapeake Bay in rural Maryland.

The silhouettes of isolated shrubs and trees frame the views and serve as the sparse focal points, but the principal building blocks are the bold horizontal planes of feathery miscanthus and pennisetum grasses, red sedum and yellow rudbeckia which interlock like a Mondrian painting. Still, all that wispy grass is not to all tastes. 'It just makes me wanna itch,' was one famous reaction.

GRAVEL GARDENS AND SUNNY TERRACES

On well-drained soils, your mind might drift towards California and the Mediterranean, where the sun-baked hills are cloaked in aromatic, narrow-leaved and silvery shrubs, interspersed with colourful bulbs, annuals and perennials. This is an obvious mood for stony, south-facing gardens, like the Aviary Terrace at Powis Castle, near Welshpool, where blue ceanothus, pink and white cistus, and yellow Jerusalem sage and Moroccan broom billow out of the red rock above rugs of helianthemum and starry white osteospermum. The high shrub content makes this a comparatively low-maintenance treatment.

Of course, you are half-way there if you have a medieval castle in your garden. But on a flat, featureless, gravelly site in East Anglia, Beth Chatto creates an equally memorable picture with the same cast of plants. Inspiration for her comes from the dry river beds of parched landscapes, so a wide gravel

'river' meanders down the view. I have seen such scenes in California and Australia, sparse and rocky, the former flushed orange with wild poppies, the latter pink with cockatoos drinking from the last puddle. Instead of rocks, Beth structures her scene with broad, rippling waves of low shrubs and evergreen bergenias, interlaced with other perennials, banked up at the sides with larger shrubs, and spiked here and there by slim conifers. If it was a private garden, you would want to domesticate it a little, if only with a table, chairs and a cream canvas parasol.

Many favourite herbs are constituents of this vegetation, and themselves make a fine theme for open, sunny gardens, whether set out in an evocative period design, with a stone basin as a centrepiece and crimson Gallica roses hanging over the box hedges, or naturalized on rocky banks as in the little 'Quarry' at The Garden House, Devon, where rugs of pink, carmine and white creeping thymes merge with helianthemums and low geraniums on ground that

↑ Fringes of mingled, meadowy planting, within a crisp formal design, are enough to inject a taste of the countryside into Gareth Hughes's Richmond garden.

has been contoured around a manmade stream and a wooden bridge (these same plants are a good cast for a paved terrace, too, which is, in effect, a rock garden on the flat).

Just below the town of Bonnieux in the Lubéron hills of southern France, the late Nicole de Vésian made a garden that has become something of a modern icon. On a series of small terraces, she sculpted the local lavender, rosemary, teucrium, box and bay into dense tapestries of clipped cushion, ball and cloud shapes. These echo the composite patterns of the pale stone walls, steps, pathways and sitting areas, so that there is integration not only with the grey-green countryside beyond but with the urban surroundings, too. (The interior of the house is also integrated: you step through the oak door off the street into a hallway carpeted in loose stones – smooth, and, I imagine, beautifully sensuous barefoot. I had been out in the heat all day, so I didn't risk taking off my shoes.)

Translated to Britain, this could be an excellent theme for gardens with a rocky outlook – coastline, say – and also for cities, where a sophisticated, year-round structure is needed. Clearly it is a formal look, but by planting asymmetrically, allowing different sizes and heights of shrub, and pruning to allow bulges, quite a playful mood can be struck.

2 — DOWN TO EARTH

Local knowledge for a gardener, as for a policeman on the beat, is everything. Are late frosts common? Does it ever stop raining? What is the soil like, and is it the same all over the garden? Where does the sun reach? There is plenty to find out. Some of it must come from patient observation, but there are short cuts.

You can take a snoop around the neighbourhood and see what everyone else is growing well. If you spot green fingers, you should introduce yourself. Gardeners love chatting about gardening, as long as it's not to a complete idiot. Similarly, you can drive to the nearest National Trust or other big garden, and get talking to the gardeners. And, if it is on your doorstep, take a tramp through the local countryside. This all helps to build a picture of the area, and gauge the potential.

CALCULATED GAMBLING

Britain's winters have been pretty benign for some years now. Elderly relatives tell you stories of annual skating parties, and you read in the history books about the Thames freezing over, with ships trapped by ice several miles out into the North Sea. Temperatures did drop devastatingly low in the south-west in 1991, but inland the last really bad winter I can remember was in 1981, my second year in my present garden, when nearby Shropshire plummeted to −26°C. Berberis, hebe, garrya, phormiums, even my privet hedge, were killed.

'Ah yes, but look what bounced back later,' says Jimmy Hancock, Powis

---

← Previous page: Blue poppies can be slippery perennials. Summer shade and moisture, and a deep fibrous soil that drains well in winter, are as important as an absence of lime. These are growing in my garden, but indulge them as I may, they do not luxuriate.

← Left: *Ceanothus* 'Puget Blue' can be killed in very hard winters, but these are now so infrequent, and as a shrub it grows so fast, that it is well worth the gamble.

Castle's head gardener at the time. 'Even shrubs like hoheria, cestrum, itea . . .' That is the right attitude. We are bound to come a cropper again one of these years, global warming notwithstanding, but that shouldn't make us overly cautious. Plants regenerate, and if they don't, well, that just means there's a gap for another juicy purchase.

So just because you live in one of the 'colder' central counties, far from the warming influence of the sea, I don't think you should feel you have to confine yourself to the safest cast of bone-hardy plants (though I will indicate the dodgier ones). I am forever bumping into the likes of red Australian bottlebrush (*Callistemon citrinus* 'Splendens') in Staffordshire, New Zealand

cabbage palm (*Cordyline australis*) in inland Sussex, and rich blue Californian *Ceanothus impressus* in the middle of Yorkshire.

This attitude puts the vast range of garden-centre plants within your grasp, and helps to realize a good few fantasies. Last year, I was standing among blue-

↑ The embryo lanterns of *Crinodendrum hookerianum* hang through the winter as hostages to fortune, and most reference books list it as half-hardy. But it has performed well in my garden for over ten years.

fronded Argentinian palms (*Trithrinax campestris*) in the middle of Martin Gibbons's garden in Ham, west of London, when a flock of green ringneck parakeets (escaped aviary birds, long naturalized around London) flew screeching into a red sunset. It could have been Mauritius.

Adventurous doesn't mean reckless. Clearly there are a lot of plants grown in the mild Gulf Stream gardens of Cornwall, Wales and Scotland that can't survive more than a few degrees below freezing, at least for any prolonged period – rocket-shaped Canary Island echiums, scented white Maddenii rhododendrons, that sort of thing. So if you are just visiting such areas, and are tempted by a new plant, it is wise to do a little research before parting with any money. Presents are another matter – you may as well give the thing a go.

Topography, however, is an important factor, and there are several locations that should have the amber lights flashing. Inland gardens at high altitude, over say 500ft/150m, have markedly colder and longer winters (though they are often spared late frosts). Exposed gardens have the problem of wind chill. And gardens by rivers on valley floors, or in dips at the base of hills, can find themselves regularly sitting in pools of cold, damp air – the notorious 'frost pockets' of gardening parlance. In such places, even fairly tough Mediterranean shrubs like rosemary and thyme are risky.

Sudden late spring frosts menace most of us to some degree, and in inland areas you are chancing your arm with the more vulnerable sort of flowers, like those of early magnolias and rhododendrons. My annual prayer is that I will have had my fun before the frost hits. The leaves of Japanese anemones, hydrangeas and kirengeshoma are always martyrs with me, but wilted foliage is soon replaced.

Keeping track of temperatures becomes addictive. One of my father's morning rituals was to tap and re-set the barometer in the hall. From autumn to spring, mine is to check the thermometer outside the back door. The maximum–minimum sort (registering the coldest point reached in the night) gives you a much better idea of what is going on in your plot than you can deduce from TV weather reports.

HELPING PLANTS THROUGH THE WINTER

You stack the odds more in favour of the riskier plants by putting them out into the garden at a decent, rather than wimpish, size, and in spring, when they have time to establish themselves before the winter; also by choosing warmer sites. South- and west-facing walls (and rocks) absorb daytime heat and radiate it at night, and a site adjacent to a heated conservatory or greenhouse can be very snug.

This is partly how Oxford Botanic Garden manages the unlikely feat of displaying the scarlet, parrot-beaked, Brazilian coral 'tree' (*Erythrina crista-galli*) outside, in a perishing spot, smack beside the river. Its other secret is to insulate it thickly with straw, surrounded by porous plastic sheeting and chicken wire. I do the same with the half-hardy Japanese banana, *Musa basjoo*, using dry leaves instead of straw, which isn't common in town.

These weird structures can be quite a feature of a winter garden. My favourite scene is Martin Rickard's tree-fern dell in chilly Worcestershire. Only the crowns of the ferns are protected, by means of a nest of straw, shielded by sections of white polystyrene box, and all held together with farmer's binder

twine. These sit 8ft/2.5m or so off the ground, on top of the fibrous trunks. The whole place looks like a makeshift set for an early episode of *Dr Who*.

Slightly tender bulbs and fleshy-rooted perennials can be persuaded to survive winters with the help of a 6 inch/15cm blanket/mulch of leaves or bark chips. Even some of the fancier dahlias can be brought through. Purple 'Admiral Rawlings' has been outside at Powis Castle for over twenty years. The alternative treatment, of course, is to lift and store them indoors,

EXOTIC HALF-HARDY PERENNIALS
WORTH RISKING UNDER A MULCH

Alstroemeria psittacina
Amaryllis belladonna
Cosmos atrosanguineus
Dahlia merckii
Eucomis
Hedychium densiflorum 'Assam Orange',
  H. d. 'Stephen' and *H. coccineum* 'Tara'

Impatiens tinctoria
Salvia patens
Tulbaghia violacea
Zantedeschia aethiopica 'Crowborough'

somewhere cool and frost-free, in a box of moistish compost; the advantage of this being that they start into spring growth sooner and come into flower earlier.

The overhead canopy of a tree or shrub, even a gappy deciduous one, gives surprising insulation against radiation frost, and can be enough protection for a slightly delicate shrub. Jimmy Hancock successfully nurtures even bell-shaped conservatory abutilons and the exotic-leaved rice-paper plant (*Tetrapanax papyrifer*) through the Midlands winter like this. And polypropylene fibre fleece (from garden centres) can be a good overnight defence against late frosts. I use it on Japanese maples, whose leaves are also easily spoilt.

RAIN GAUGE

The amount of rain a garden receives is obviously going to please some plants more than others. Local topography produces surprising variations, but it is safe to say that the south-eastern counties are dry, often getting less than 20 inches/50cm a year, very little of that falling in summer. So unless you have a cool, moist site, there is no point struggling to create a lush Asian woodland with plants like blue poppies, candelabra primulas, large-leaved

← | The South African bulb *Tulbaghia violacea* is proving hardy for me under a gravel mulch.

rhododendrons and tree ferns, which want a humid atmosphere as well as a retentive soil. Unless you are prepared to irrigate. For tree ferns, that means running drip nozzles into their crowns. In London, the low rainfall problem is aggravated by the drying heat of all those walls.

By contrast, the far western counties, from Cornwall up to Wester Ross, can get 40, 50, even over 60 inches/1–1.5m a year, which is hopeless for many Mediterranean plants, especially those with silver leaves (New Zealanders, like senecio, astelia, and celmisia, can be good substitutes), and even for many roses, which succumb to fungal diseases.

These are the extremes. Here on the Welsh border, with a decent average rainfall of over 30 inches/75cm, I like to assume I can grow almost anything I want, if I can find it the right position. Big-leaved rhodos don't luxuriate or flower well for me, but as long as they are not in competition with tree roots they can still sprout leaf-buds the size of surface-to-air missile shells (the woolly grey and shrimp pink of *R. macabeanum* is one of the wonders of June). My lavenders are as appetizing as old dishcloths in winter, and my bergenia leaves don't turn crimson like Beth Chatto's, but if I give them the sunniest spots I can find, they put on a brave face at flowering time.

Within your garden there will also be micro-habitats. The rainshadows of walls and trees offer congenial homes for plants that prefer staying dry, as do overhanging eaves. I have seen Mexican agaves brought through winters like this (planting them at a slant helps, so water can't lodge and freeze in their leaf joints). And for plants that like being wet, there is always that leaking drainpipe and the dripping overflow from the rainwater butt; you can also sink pond-liner 18 inches/45cm under the soil, speared with a few drainage holes.

CONSERVING RAINFALL

Most plants like to keep their roots moist in summer, so I do believe in giving borders a mulch. This means putting down a layer of something over the surface of the soil, to reduce evaporation by the sun. This also has the labour-saving benefit of drastically suppressing weed growth. For plants from rocky habitats, the ideal material is, of course, rough gravel, which keeps stems dry at the base. It should be 1–2 inches/2.5–5cm deep. You get a more natural effect by mixing different grades, from quite large stone chippings to grit. Glass is a trendy alternative (to be avoided).

For woodland and meadow plants, mulches are more ephemeral, being composed of waste vegetable material which slowly rots away. They are best spread in early spring, about 3 inches/8cm deep. You want something fairly coarse, not too rich, and cheap. I use homemade leafmould for the woodlanders, and homemade compost for the meadow plants. Composted bark and green waste, from garden centres and some local authorities, are good substitutes. Grass clippings look and smell awful. Bark chips give too much of a manicured appearance, like one of those roundabouts sponsored by the local factory, studded with rocks and heather.

Dead leaves make a fine mulch in the rougher corners of the garden, saving you the trouble of collecting them. The copper tints of fallen beech leaves complement evergreen shrubs particularly well, and rhododendrons love sitting in their own litter. (I wish those in charge of local parks would recognize this,

← I rarely get flowers from *Rhododendron macabeanum*, but given buds like these, it would be churlish to complain.

and not strip their shrubberies to compacted bare soil every autumn; it looks so depressing.) Year by year, the blanket of leaves is topped up of its own accord, and periodically you can harvest the underlying mould, and so reduce the depth. Blackbirds particularly enjoy this *laissez-faire* approach, and it gives hedgehogs somewhere to hibernate.

WIND DEFENCES

Brought up by the sea, on the island of Anglesey, I remember times when the wind was so strong it took two people to get the back door shut. On most days there was a bracing breeze, and the only place you could calmly enjoy the island's high sunshine levels was in crouched position behind the garden wall. Quite how the planners of American cities could have been daft enough to set out their streets on open-ended grid patterns, inviting the wind to channel its energy into ferocious tunnels (freezing in winter), is a mystery.

Wind is not much fun for plants, either. Grasses sway beautifully, but other things get torn, snapped, desiccated and frost-scorched. So shelter is important for gardens, and creates a warmer, more hospitable environment.

Walls stop the wind completely, but only for a short distance. The wind is buffeted upwards like a wave, only to come down again with a crash. More efficient is a barrier that lets wind through, but slows it down. Fifty per cent porosity is considered ideal, and this gives good protection over a distance equivalent to ten times its height. Gappy fences, like hazel and willow, are thus a little better than solid ones in exposed places. Along my Oxford terrace, the larch-lap type would buckle and rock its posts in every gale, producing a chorus of hammerings and curses from the neighbours the next day.

But for a decent height of barrier, a combination of evergreen and deciduous trees, bolstered low down by shrubs and hedges, is the answer. There are numerous tough trees to choose from but invariably you are impatient for results:

ATTRACTIVE, FAST-GROWING SHELTER TREES

- *Alnus cordata*
- *Betula pendula*
- *Cupressus macrocarpa*
- *Fraxinus angustifolia* 'Raywood'
- *Pinus muricata*
- *Pinus radiata*

- *Pinus sylvestris*
  Prunus avium
- *Quercus rubra*
- *Salix caprea*
- *Sequoiadendron giganteum*
- *Thuja plicata* 'Atrovirens'

Tree magnolias emerged from the Great Storm of October 1987 with flying colours, and are now being used in National Trust shelter belts in the milder counties. But really they are best inside the garden, so their flowers don't get ripped. For inland areas, my choice would be *M. sprengeri* var. *diva*, which gives you an explosion of rose-pink waterlilies in April. Go to the Savill Garden, Windsor, and be dumbstruck. But ask questions before buying one. After a five-year wait, my blooms turned out to be white, and rather pathetic: clearly a seedling, not a cutting. Grrr.

↑ Red oak, *Quercus rubra* (*left*), and sea buckthorn, *Hippophae rhamnoides* (*right*), make handsome shelter plants.

If you are in your garden for the long term, and it is fairly large, you can use fast-growing trees simply as a nurse crop, interplanting them with tough but slow species, like many of the oaks and limes. Gradually, the nurse trees are felled. In this case you can even include poplars and Leyland cypress (dread words) in the mix.

A temporary fence of polyethylene mesh, as used in garden centres, helps plants establish on exposed sites. But, in any case, it is best to put in fairly short plants, which can develop sturdy root anchors in pace with their top growth.

At a lower height, there are also many fast-growing, wind-resistant shrubs and hedging plants. Again, these can be used either as permanent residents, or as temporary fillers to nurse along slow plants like yew, box and holly:

GOOD QUICK SHELTER SHRUBS

- *Berberis* × *stenophylla*
- *Cotoneaster lacteus*
- *Elaeagnus* × *ebbingei*
- *Escallonia rubra* 'Crimson Spire'
- *Hippophae rhamnoides*
- *Prunus lusitanica*
- *Salix alba* subsp. *vitellina*
- *Salix alba* subsp. *vitellina* 'Britzensis'
- *Sambucus nigra* 'Guincho Purple'
- *Spartium junceum*
- *Spiraea* 'Arguta'
- *Viburnum opulus* 'Compactum'

CAR NOISE

Plants are not very efficient insulation against car noise. You have only to visit the RHS garden at Wisley to see how little impact that belt of trees and shrubbery has on the din of the adjacent A3. An acoustics expert told me that you need an evergreen thicket at least 25ft/7.5m deep to gain even a 25 per cent reduction in noise.

By contrast, a solid wall, fence, or earth mound can achieve twice that, as long as it's high enough (6ft/2m minimum) and close to the noise source. If this is impossible, similar defences inside the garden will at least create small, localized pockets of calm. In addition, you can counter the noise with the sound of water – a large enough waterfall will drown out almost anything.

SUN AND SHADE

I am surprised when friends can't tell me, without scratching their heads, which way their garden faces. I don't see how you can organize any sensible layout, let alone plant anything, without knowing roughly how much light each wall, border and open space receives.

Once you have found out, every site becomes an opportunity. Given a gloomy wall, I don't waste a moment lamenting all the roses and wisterias I can't grow. Instead, I think of all those giant-leaved hydrangeas and scarlet-berried actaeas, and the prospect of *Clematis* 'Miss Bateman' sporting lime-green stripes on her white petals – which never appear in sunlight.

Areas facing south and south-west are, of course, the sunniest, exposed to a good few hours of mid-morning to mid-afternoon heat. But south-east is equally congenial; indeed, the loss of heat on summer afternoons can be a blessing. And there are few sun-lovers I wouldn't grow on a west-facing site, given unobstructed afternoon light.

Less than two hours of strong sunshine, and you have to assume you are dealing with shade, or at least part-shade. East-facing walls and the ground immediately adjacent to them, which get only the weaker morning rays, are in this category: the combination of gentle sun and coolness here is ideal for many fussy plants, such as gentians.

As you move around to the north, you have to start dropping almost everything but woodlanders. The choice of species is still overwhelming. Indeed, you link up with much the same cast of plants as you might use in the dappled light under tree branches – though under trees I find it is best to avoid tall, vertical shrubs, which invariably develop an annoying lean.

The two more restrictive sorts of shade are, first, dark shade, which you get under heavy deciduous tree canopies (it is often possible to alleviate matters by thinning branches and removing lower limbs) and in the gaps between buildings. And second, dry shade, which is particularly associated with surface-rooting trees, like beech, and with evergreens, like holm oak and yew. *Nil desperandum*, as my Latin teacher used to write on my school reports; I will make a few suggestions later on. Meanwhile, one solution might be containers or raised beds, which at least give plants a deep, moist root-run.

TESTING YOUR SOIL

Happily, the vast majority of plants, including almost all perennials, are not particularly fussy about the acidity or alkalinity of the soil. I am forever travelling back home with a bootload of plants gleaned one week from a nursery on acid Devon moorland, and the next from one on Cotswold limestone, and I expect them to glow with health for years to come.

But you do need to know what you've got. And by doing a pH test in various places, you can often find quite big variations – such as next to lime-mortared walls. I admit I have never actually done a pH test in my garden, for the flourishing rhododendrons, and the eruptions of bracken through the paving cracks, were a pretty good indication that my sandy loam was acid. You can be fooled, though, for someone can easily have fiddled with the soil, especially in the vegetable patch.

Nick and Pam Coote have visitors drooling at the sight of a pair of gentian-blue hydrangeas ('Générale Vicomtesse de Vibraye') either side of their front door. Mophead hydrangeas, whose flowers react to acidity like litmus paper, should be pink, or at best red, in limy Oxford. But here they are grown in half-barrels in acid compost, watered with rainwater, and given liberal doses of hydrangea blueing compound from the garden centre.

I have come across a few plants that dislike my acid soil, including white Madonna lily (*Lilium candidum*) and the big blue-flowered scabious 'Clive Greaves'. Under beech trees, where the ground is very acid, my hellebores are

→ | *Pieris japonica* 'Firecrest' is part of the large tribe of ericaceous shrubs which dislike limy soils. But there is no problem growing them in half-barrels filled with acid compost, placed along shady pathways.

also unhappy. Instead of expanding into fat clumps, they tend to shrink from year to year; I have now started adding lime to the soil around them.

Owners of alkaline gardens have quite a list of plants to avoid (though many of them are happy enough under neutral to slightly alkaline conditions), predominantly:

LIME-HATERS

TREES

◊ Halesia	◊ Nyssa	◊ Styrax
◊ Nothofagus	◊ Stewartia	◊ Taxodium

SHRUBS

• Calluna	• Erica (some)	• Kalmia
• Camellia	◊ Eucryphia	• Pieris
• Crinodendron	◊ Fothergilla	• Rhododendron (including
• Desfontainea	• Gaultheria (including	azaleas)
◊ Disanthus	Pernettya)	◊ Vaccinium

PERENNIALS

Gentiana sino-ornata	Lilium auratum/speciosum/	Meconopsis
	Oriental Hybrids	

But even given a seriously alkaline soil, like chalk, there is no need to feel cheated. You have only to go to Highdown, on the chalk cliffs above Goring-on-Sea in Sussex, to see the potential: naturalized tulips; rivers of blue and white anemones; bearded irises and tree peonies; roses and lilacs . . . Quite a sight, especially in April and May.

PREPARING YOUR SOIL

The traditional gardening manuals make it sound rotten luck to have a soil that, in its structure, falls far short of the chocolate-cake ideal. And to bang home the point, there is always an image of some lonely soul ploughing his furrow, double-digging and heaving on the manure, striving for perfection.

The message from today's naturalistic gardeners is that there is a cast of plants suited to every sort of soil. Indeed, radical 'improvement' may even be counter-productive, making the ground so water-retentive and fertile that many plants, unaccustomed to such excess in the wild, become over-vigorous, high-maintenance, and even short-lived.

On the other hand, you do want each habitat to be as congenial as possible, and your garden to offer plenty of opportunity for interesting planting. So the best approach is to see exactly what you have got; let it steer you towards the cast of plants best adapted to it; and when you do tweak it, to widen your scope, amend it wisely.

A soil that is friable, decently moist in summer, and decently drained in winter, can obviously accommodate a very broad spectrum of plants. And, happily, many gardens have one. All you really have to do to prepare it for planting is to dig it over (or rotavate with a deeply penetrating cultivator – I'd get a contractor to do it).

But no digging until you have eliminated all perennial weeds, of course. A systemic weedkiller based on glyphosate (Roundup) will polish off most weeds, if it is applied when plants are in full and active growth, in spring and summer. But it may take more than one application, over a period of months. Indeed, in the case of horsetail and Japanese knotweed, the devil's own weeds, you can be talking years. Bashing their stems with a stick before spraying allows more poison to be absorbed – and feels good.

Woodland plants like a soil particularly rich in humus, so in the shadier areas, where you are going to grow them, it may be an idea to fork in some fibrous organic matter (leafmould, composted bark or composted greenwaste) before planting. In the sunniest areas, where dry habitat plants are going to live, you may want to add some sharp horticultural grit (from builders' merchants) to give that extra bit of drainage.

On light soil, sand or gravel, or where the climate is dry, a boost of humus right through the garden is sensible. It improves water retention and gives plants a good start. I used well-rotted manure on the sandier parts of mine. But it is heavy, and nasty perennial weeds like couch grass can arrive with it.

Mushroom compost, which should also be stacked until well-rotted, has an attractive texture, though its high alkalinity rules it out on very alkaline soils, or where acid-loving woodlanders are to be grown. Beth Chatto used it for her new gravel garden. Other good all-round contenders are, again, either your own compost and leafmould, or bought-in composted bark and greenwaste.

According to the Royal Horticultural Society, peat's usefulness as a soil improver has proved 'at best, cosmetic'. In overdose, it can even be quite dangerous. Back in the late 1970s, when I started gardening, it was used for everything short of grouting. Planting holes were packed with it. But after the Great Storm of 1987, I was shown a tree that had blown down at Winkworth Arboretum in Surrey. Its pocket of peat was still intact. It had dried out, and never re-wetted, so creating an area of instability which the roots had scrupulously avoided.

Similarly, container plants grown in peat-based compost can be very vulnerable when transferred into border soil, especially in spells of dry weather. Before planting, I tease the roots out and shake off as much of the peat as I can.

And of course the other major worry with peat is the damage its extraction causes to rare bog habitats, and their flora and fauna. It doesn't feel good to know you are gardening at the expense of the environment. Some peatland habitats are not endangered, and can support extraction, but in the garden centre it is hard to discern the source and make an informed decision. So, as well as not using raw peat, I have now also stopped using 'multipurpose' peat-based potting composts, opting instead for John Innes soil-based compost and the new peat-free mixes coming on to the market.

Heavy clay soil is tricky, easily compacted and stickily unworkable when wet. I have just been considering the best way of tackling it in a Hampshire garden recently bought by my friends George and Lucinda Tindley. As Lady Farm shows, there is a range of trees, shrubs and perennials that will accept it just as it is, as long as it is not badly waterlogged (when you might need land drains). Given a sunny slope, and the incorporation of sharp grit into the top spit (say, two parts to five parts soil), this range can even be extended to Mediterranean plants. Early autumn is a good time to dig it over. Mushroom compost, which contains the clay-breaker gypsum, is another excellent additive.

But the Tindleys' garden is on the flat, and they want to grow some of the plants that Blackthorn Nursery, the hellebore and daphne specialists, are offering up the road. I think the best option is the raised bed approach, gently working some grit and gravel into the clay topsoil (maybe removing some of it first), and then spreading a layer of imported topsoil above it.

Bringing in topsoil is a tempting policy on shallow stony and chalk soils, too. And definitely in extreme urban situations, where the ground is exhausted to dust or reduced to a rubbly subsoil.

NURTURING YOUR SOIL

In the wild, nobody goes around feeding plants. But there is a continual recycling of nutrients going on, as leaves and top growth fall and decay, and get worked on by micro-organisms. By cutting down and clearing borders, you are continually removing this store of organic matter, so somehow it needs to be replaced.

Light spring mulches of compost and leafmould, applied when the ground is moist, are the ideal method. They add small amounts of nutrient, and give plants access to the nutrients already in the soil by making it moister. And there are plenty of nutrients in most garden soils. Rain tops up nitrogen levels, polluted rain alarmingly so.

Whenever I replant a tired area of border, I top up the humus level. And every few years, also in early spring, I give borders a dusting of blood, fish and bonemeal, a slow-release organic fertilizer which, I hope, will address any deficiencies and imbalances – particularly in the gravelly areas, which don't get any compost or leafmould.

Here and there, you want an over-the-top performance, and given additional rations many plants will respond in the right way. Hedges, for instance, need to be kept vigorously leafy; showy, manmade plants like roses, delphiniums and sweet peas need plenty of sustenance if they are to reach their full potential; and from fruit and veg, you want high yields. So I give these spots an annual spring application of blood, fish and bone, and, for the roses and the greedier type of annual and perennial, extra doses of quick-acting liquid fertilizer.

My favourite is liquid seaweed extract (Maxicrop). I think, as did the late Geoff Hamilton, that it has magical powers – and its smell transports me back to my seaside childhood. Used as a foliage spray and root drench on fruit trees and bushes – or on anything that looks a bit peaky – it not only produces a healthy green, but seems to ward off disease. Researchers are currently investigating this.

For plants in containers, where nutrients get flushed out by the watering-can, I use mainly Maxicrop's high potash (tomato) fertilizer, which is balanced more towards flower and fruit production. For foliage plants, you want a feed with a higher nitrogen content, which you can alternate with Maxicrop Original seaweed growth stimulant.

MAKING COMPOST AND LEAFMOULD

Homemade compost and leafmould are becoming a litany in this chapter, but I urge all my friends to get cracking on their heaps the moment they move house. Plumbing and decorating can wait.

My three compost bins are each 4 by 4 by 5ft/1.25 × 1.25 × 1.5m high, with breeze-block sides, slatted wooden fronts, and plastic sheeting roofs. Waste materials from the garden – grass clippings, prunings, branch shreddings, weeds (but not the roots of invasive perennial weeds), vegetable peelings and wood ash – are piled on as they become available. When the heap is full, it is turned and thoroughly tossed like a salad, so there are no thick layers of anything. It is left for a couple of months, and then turned again, with fresh grass clippings, or some other activator like 6x, added as a high nitrogen source to reactivate the rotting. It is ready a couple of months later.

There are faster and better ways of making compost, but they require you to be more organized than I am. Pay a visit to the Henry Doubleday Research Association (HDRA) in Ryton-on-Dunsmore, just off the M6 near Coventry, for enlightenment. Don't probe too deeply into what they put in their heaps, or you will be put off the tea shop's excellent homegrown carrot cake.

To make leafmould, I was once told that all I had to do was fill a bin bag with leaves, stab it repeatedly with a fork for aeration, tie it up, and wait two years. I did. It was like opening a time capsule. The missing piece of information was that the leaves needed to be moist.

Now I have two proper leafmould bins, which are simply three-sided post and chicken-mesh cubicles, again 4 by 4 by 5ft/1.25 × 1.25 × 1.5m high, open to the elements. Most of the leaves are collected off the lawn with the mower, so they are chewed up a little, which helps to speed up the decomposition. Leaves from elsewhere I often pass through the shredder. But if you are not in a hurry, none of this is necessary. It is, however, a good idea to mix in grass clippings as an activator. The crumbly soil-like product is usually ready after eighteen months. There is no need to turn the heaps.

TRYING TO BE ORGANIC

'I can see that the world might be a better place if there were fewer chemicals thrown about, but as the owner of a small town garden where everything needs to look good and healthy, I find it hard to be completely organic,' Anthony Goff, my literary agent, confessed to me. I do, too.

Of course, with a more relaxed, naturalistic style of gardening, you are not striving for showcase perfection. In the wild, plants are seldom unblemished. What's more, I love to see the garden alive with animals. But you don't want pests and diseases playing havoc. So I do use aluminium sulphate granules (Growing Success) against slugs and snails around lilies and hostas. Reputedly harmless to all other wildlife (and listed in organic gardening catalogues), I have used this remedy for many years, and the garden continues to support an enormous frog population, as well as thrushes. Sharp grit is an alternative, but that can be obtrusive.

If I get a serious outbreak of aphids or other pest, and the ladybirds and other predators don't seem to be dealing with it, I tackle the job either with my fingers or with one of the organic insecticides, such as insecticidal soft soap, recommended by HDRA. If the same plant has the problem badly year after year – lupins, for instance – I dig them out.

I hunt for my *bête noire*, the vine weevil, at midnight, with a miner's torch strapped to my head. The nocturnal adults are dull, grey-black beetles (not shiny black like ground beetles, which are valuable garden predators) and bite half-moon notches around the leaves of perennials and shrubs. This isn't so bad, but they are all female (reproducing by parthenogenesis), and as they go about their business they drop eggs.

These turn into fat white, brown-headed grubs, which gorge on the roots of fleshy plants. Plants in pots are frequently killed by them. The grubs explode spectacularly between the fingers, but if you don't want to re-pot things frequently, you can use a biological control, in the form of a nematode, or parasitic worm. If vine weevils are not in your garden already, they are surely on their way. One tried to climb into my car at an M5 service station recently.

For rusts and blackspot diseases there are no organic remedies. And they seem to be plaguing an increasing number of plants these days. Removing affected leaves quickly, giving vulnerable plants plenty of air circulation, and a periodic spray with liquid seaweed extract can help. But if not, and the plant is something you really do want to keep, you will have to turn to a fungicide as a last resort, alternating two or three different ones so the plants don't build up resistance. Sulphur, used as a powder or spray, is the approved organic treatment for powdery mildew.

True organic gardeners do not use weedkillers. New ground is cleared of weeds by means of black polythene sheeting, paths are kept clean with flame-guns, and mulching and close planting helps prevent weed outbreaks. Certainly

I adhere to this last principle; if you can see bare soil in my garden by June, something must have died. But often a weedkiller is the most practical way of clearing weeds from soil, drive or lawn (though I much prefer a community of little wildflowers in my sward to a sterile green billiard table); similarly, when you get an eruption of bindweed or ground-elder in the border or the hedge.

Weedkillers based on glyphosate are among the least toxic, but though glyphosate itself decomposes rapidly on contact with the soil, I am told that the additives combined with it can leave some residue. New formulations are being developed which address this problem.

3 — APPROACHES TO PLANTING

Before plunging any deeper into border planning, it is a good idea to decide how much of a design challenge you want to set yourself, and how much time you can give to maintenance. It is very easy to bite off more than you can chew – says I, with bulging mouthful.

KEEPING IT SIMPLE

It seems to me that there are easier and harder ways to plant a garden, and most of us instinctively choose the hardest. We grow too many plants. It is obvious really, but the more ingredients you add to a border, the trickier it is both to manage and to make sense of visually. So, when friends ask me how some piece of planting could be improved, I usually tell them to throw out ninety per cent of the plants. I enjoy the reaction. (I would like to have seen Vita Sackville-West's face when she asked Edwin Lutyens for suggestions, after taking him on a tour of her first garden at Long Barn, near Sevenoaks. 'Move,' he replied.)

Still, it is worth reminding yourself how potent and memorable the simplest planting schemes can be: a bank of daffodils, say, or a wall smothered in white rambler rose. More sophisticated is the long, narrow stream of purple lavender, speared at intervals by dark, vertical Irish yews, that divides two sections of lawn at Mottisfont Abbey, Hampshire. Rich purple and grass green is an arresting colour mix. So is scarlet and green. At Penpergwm Lodge, Abergavenny, Catriona Boyle has planted a pergola entirely in green vines,

← Previous page: Variegated dogwood, *Cornus alternifolia* 'Argentea', and the moisture-loving tree *Cercidiphyllum japonicum* set a simple theme of contrasting shapes at The Garden House. The free-for-all of Welsh poppies and campanulas, colonizing the crevices, lightens the mood.

with a fat clump of sword-leaved *Crocosmia* 'Lucifer' at the base of each post:
a fine partnership even out of flower, although there is nothing there in winter.

Several Februarys ago, I went to a garden in woods near Seattle given over to
hellebores. Four acres of hellebores. Its owner, Elfi Rahr, was completely
besotted with them, so much so that after eventually agreeing to sell some of
her offspring to a local nursery, she experienced such pangs that she went and
bought them back. (The trouble is that every hellebore is different, with its own
little personality.)

It was a drizzly day, but the garden was a wonderland, a torrent of nodding
heads flowing down banks and around tree trunks to the edge of a lake, quiet
enough still to be fished by bald eagles. Her simple, unmanicured approach was
very much in the spirit of the place, unlike her neighbours over the fence who
had suburbanized their plot with little lawns and flower-beds – not a leaf out of
place. 'You can tell they are dental hygienists,' chuckled Elfi.

Another garden that haunts me is Lorna McMahon's in Galway, on the west
coast of Ireland. It comprises a string of water gardens inside an old hazel
copse. From glinting, peaty streams and pools, and sweeps of colourful astilbes
and primulas, you walk into the dappled, mossy world of crooked hazel stems,

↑ At Lady Farm, a restrained passage of birches, hostas and *Allium hollandicum* serves as a
sorbet between rich servings of colourful border.

sheeted with bluebells in spring, and with the remnants of stone walls snaking under the green canopy. One day, I shall plant my own bluebell nuttery.

But at the very least, a garden needs passages of simplicity. One intricate border after another is a bit much to take. Somebody on my bookshelf (I can't remember who) compares it to serving up one rich plateful after another at dinner. Periodically, you yearn for a sorbet. An expanse of lawn, gravel or evergreen shrubs can provide it; in one Chelsea garden, the designer Christopher Bradley-Hole has planted an entire bed with clipped globes of box, set against a sensuous wall of warm terracotta (achieved, in this instance, by brushing marble and mineral dust on to smooth plaster).

Among flowers, cool colours make the best refreshers, and a long run of a single species calms a scene nicely. Successive lines of catmint, blue irises and lavender terminate the mingled terrace planting at Gravetye Manor, Sussex. At Crathes Castle, Aberdeenshire, mixed beds of crimson roses, purple-leaved shrubs, and orange and yellow perennials are interrupted by a stone path, flanked by swags of old chain, foaming in nothing but lime-green *Alchemilla mollis*. And in a garden in Connecticut, James van Sweden has filled the view from the sitting-room with the most enormous bolt of white Japanese anemones (*A. × hybrida* 'Honorine Jobert') I have ever seen – well framed by the window's blue-grey paintwork. These anemones are in flower from July to October, but further action can easily be programmed by interplanting with bulbs, such as snowdrops or daffodils.

Visually, perennials do gain immeasurably from being grown in a decent-sized drift, but I would only sacrifice the space to plants that either bloom for a very long time, or have appealing foliage. A hosta bed, for example, can be a stunning feature in shade, slugs permitting, with the blue and white-variegated forms gradually blended into the greens and yellows (again, bulbs could be massed around them in spring). The tall, blue-leaved plume poppies, *Macleaya*

cordata and *M. microcarpa* 'Coral Plume', create an equally impressive foliage sweep in sun.

In moist ground at Inverewe, near Ullapool, the parasol leaves of *Darmera peltata* line the woodland paths like low hedges. While at Kerdalo, in Brittany, rivulets of carmine and pink candelabra primulas lead into a green gulch, entirely filled with the filigree shapes of shuttlecock ferns (*Matteucia*), backed by the giant rhubarb foliage of *Gunnera manicata*.

AREAS THAT LOOK AFTER THEMSELVES

To free time to spend on pleasant jobs, you need to wriggle out of some of the chores. There are bound to be places where it is no fun gardening, such as slap beside the road, on a steep bank, or, in my case, in the dry rooty ground around the holly bushes, where my posterior gets stabbed every time I crouch down. Here, simplicity in the form of minimal maintenance, weed-suppressing ground-cover shrubs and perennials is the answer.

Lesser periwinkle, *Vinca minor*, is one of the neatest low evergreens for sun or shade. At Great Dixter, Sussex, Christopher Lloyd mixes blue and white forms at the base of a yew hedge (always a tricky location), strimming them every three years, in winter. I do the same with greater periwinkle, *Vinca major*. Of the Mongol horde persuasion, this is a much harder plant to restrain and extract, so shouldn't be introduced anywhere very sensitive. But if, like mine, your hedge doesn't reach to the ground, but rather exposes varicosed feet and knobbly legs, then the taller evergreen habit of this species comes in handy; it grows strongly even in a dry rain shadow. Both periwinkles have fetching variegated versions.

Other thick evergreen duvets are provided by pachysandra (which needs acid soil); ivies (which are the best bet in very dark, dry, permanent shade), and the low rush *Luzula sylvatica*. At Bodnant the shady woodland banks are cloaked in this lawn substitute, which has to be strimmed just once a year, in autumn. In the gloom around my hollies I use the white-splashed deadnettle, *Lamium*

← | Japanese anemone (*left*) and shuttlecock fern deserve to be grown in a generous drift.

galeobdolon 'Florentinum'. It looks very chirpy leaping about in copper leaf litter, but is more of a thug than you might think: German research reveals that, over time, it is capable of out-competing and eradicating ground-elder (I reckon acanthus could, too; I notice it is defeating winter heliotrope at Powis Castle).

Of the deciduous ground-covers, my favourite is the hardy geranium *G. macrorrhizum*, especially in its form 'Album', which has white flowers from deep pink buds. It engulfs the trunks of my apple trees. At Wakehurst Place, Sussex, the creeping knotweed, *Persicaria affinis* 'Superba', makes a beautiful impression on the banks of the dell, a little forest of dark and pale pink bottlebrushes for months on end. And in Monet's garden at Giverny, I was much taken with the broad rugs of variegated ground-elder lining the paths. This is a plant that has to be sold under the disguise of its Latin name, *Aegopodium podagraria* 'Variegatum'. Once inside the garden, it takes few prisoners, but at least it moves as a cohort and you can watch what it is up to. I have never seen it revert to green.

LOW GROUND-COVERING PLANTS

SHADE

Aegopodium	Epimedium	Luzula	Symphytum
Alchemilla	Geranium	Pachysandra	Tiarella
Asperula	Lamium	Persicaria	Vinca
Blechnum (ferns)			

SUN

Acaena	Geranium	Nepeta	Phlomis
Ajuga	Liriope	Persicaria	Stachys
Alchemilla			

Given sufficient winter light, you can usually install bulbs underneath these ground-covers to extend the interest – daffodils under geranium and ivy, Spanish bluebells under lesser periwinkle, that sort of thing. And with the addition of larger shrubs, you have the recipe here for very attractive, low-maintenance borders, even whole gardens. But the plantings do need fizz –

unexpected solo plants, brilliant flower colour, wacky ornament, dramatic leaves – if they aren't to look like a municipal cop-out.

SIDE-STEPPING THE THUGS

On the whole, tree and shrub plantings are less demanding than plantings of perennials. There is less exposed soil for weeds to colonize, and the plants don't need any spadework. But there are a number of ways of reducing the work load among perennials – beyond those I have already mentioned, such as the use of mulches to suffocate weed seedlings.

For a start, you can save yourself a lot of trouble by not mixing the more invasive plants with the more sedentary. The worst offenders are those that colonize by running roots. With them, the best approach is to contain them among shrubs and ground-cover plants. *Euphorbia griffithii* 'Fireglow' has been attempting to murder (by sending up underground spears) my clumps of yellow *Phlomis russeliana* for ten years now without success. Both bloom freely. ('Dixter' is less invasive.) And at Dunham Massey, Cheshire, pink *Clerodendrum bungei* is teamed up with the equally invasive tree poppy, *Romneya coulteri*, achieving a very handsome leaf partnership, and two seasons of flowers.

ATTRACTIVE PLANTS WITH INVASIVE ROOTS

Alstroemeria aurea	Epilobium angustifolium var.	Macleaya
Artemisia ludoviciana	album	Mentha
Clerodendrum bungei	Euphorbia cyparissias	Nepeta sibirica
Crocosmia × crocosmiiflora	Euphorbia griffithii	Romneya coulteri
(montbretia)	Lysimachia punctata	Rubus idaeus 'Aureus'

Plants that produce copious quantities of seedlings also need to be treated with caution. You may think you have shaved them all to the ground before they drop their load, but there will always be one or two that you have missed. The best policy is often to let them sow themselves into areas of paving, where the excess is easily weed-killed out, or, as with the runners above, to site them in beds of shrubs and tough perennials which can look after themselves. Sometimes it is fun just to let them rip, as bronze fennel does through the blue and yellow borders of roses, euphorbias, forget-me-nots, alchemilla, solidago and golden grasses at Hadspen, Somerset.

ATTRACTIVE PLANTS WITH ABUNDANT SEED

Alchemilla	Corydalis lutea	Lythrum salicaria	Tanacetum
Aquilegia	Foeniculum vulgare	Myrrhis odorata	parthenium
Campanula	Geranium	Rumex sanguineus	
trachelium	pyrenaicum	Silene dioica	

Some plants are just not worth the trouble, though. Unless you have a sand-dune to stabilize, I wouldn't bother with any of the running grasses. There are equally attractive clump-forming ones. My worst pests at home are yellow and orange Welsh poppies, *Meconopsis cambrica*, which I inherited, and pink claytonia and shimmery silverweed (*Potentilla anserina*), which I stupidly introduced myself. Fortunately we have now got rid of the creeping bamboo (*Sasa veitchii*) I stole from the parrot house at Chester Zoo, but only after digging up two stretches of paved path to find its secret lairs. I failed to appreciate I needed the parrots, too; only their constant gnawing can keep it in check.

TROUBLESOME PLANTS BEST AVOIDED

Allium triquetrum	Claytonia sibirica	Ornithogalum	Potentilla anserina
Campanula	Leymus arenarus	umbellatum	Saponaria officinalis
rapunculoides	Meconopsis	Petasites	Sasa
Cerastium	cambrica	Phalaris	
tomentosum		arundinacea 'Picta'	

→   *Anthemis tinctoria* 'E. C. Buxton' puts on a tremendous show, but needs cutting down after flowering, and regular division in spring, if it is not to die out. It is more persistent on poor, well-drained soil.

AVOIDING BARE SOIL

Nature, as we know, abhors a vacuum, and weed troubles are at their worst in beds where plants are separated by empty soil, especially when this is regularly disturbed by digging, which activates the enormous bank of weed seeds lying dormant. Here at home, most of my borders are only forked if I have been standing on them, and in the process caused compaction. Generally, I try to stay off them as much as possible, relying on the mulches and worm activity to keep them aerated (stepping stones help me navigate through the wider beds). I may have to do some hoeing in spring, but by June my hope is that the plants will have knitted together into a solid enough blanket to give weeds little opportunity.

However, there are certain categories of plants that do require regular intervention. A number of the more glamorous, highly-bred perennials, notably hybrid phloxes, delphiniums, monardas, daylilies, crocosmias, and bearded iris varieties, need dividing every couple of years to keep them flowering well (though their parent species can often go indefinitely without disturbance). Half-hardy and short-lived plants, like yellow *Anthemis tinctoria*, most tulips, dahlias, many lilies and penstemons, require regular renewal. And the soil has to be tilled for annuals and biennials that are to be bedded out or, like poppies, nigella, cornflowers and larkspur, sown *in situ* in autumn or spring.

The full-time gardener can cope with these sorts of plants dotted right through the border, but for the rest of us it makes sense to keep them to certain, accessible areas – near paths, close to the front of borders – which are designated as high-maintenance hot spots. This doesn't mean ghettoizing them. (Though for artistic reasons, purist German designers do advise segregating the very fancy plants from the wilder ones. I wouldn't make it a rule. An eruption of tropical purple canna leaves among the hardy geraniums can be fun.)

I try to curb my desire for masses of high-maintenance plants, but it is hard when they include so many of the more exciting species, and when I come

home hotfoot from an inspiring garden like Tom Hobbs and Brent Beattie's, overlooking Vancouver Bay in Canada. The house is an unlikely one for its location, an amazing pinkish-terracotta Spanish-style villa which, as they say, looks as if it ought to have belonged to some fading silent-screen Hollywood goddess. Windowsills drip with begonias, paths are bedded out with juicy succulent echeverias, the yellow trumpets of brugmansia arch over the blue-tiled outdoor hot tub. Every bed is a piece of theatre. But it is a small garden, there is time to tweak and polish, and it is their owners' passion. 'I'm going to have one of those plants, even if I have to go to gaol,' Tom will mutter, when hearing of something new, rare and mouth-watering.

The traditional herbaceous border is also associated with a great deal of fiddly and time-consuming staking. But from Alan Bloom's experiments with island beds at Bressingham, Norfolk, from the 1950s onwards, we know that this can be considerably reduced if plants are sited in a more natural way. In the wild, most tall perennials grow in bright, open positions. If they have something solid immediately behind them, like a hedge, a wall or a big shrub, they have a tendency to stretch for the light, by growing taller and developing a lean – in turn, affecting the plants below them.

What's more, because they are not exposed to much wind, the young stems are not encouraged to thicken. Come a sudden heavy downpour, and everything is flattened.

So the contemporary approach of growing tall perennials in more meadowy ways, among their own kind and with grasses, in preference to shrubs, and not having them in one-sided, steeply graded tiers, does help. But it won't cut out all staking, especially if you are growing some of the notoriously top-heavy and vulnerable plants, such as delphiniums, dahlias, peonies, oriental poppies, lilies, galegas, and alstroemerias. The bellflower, *Campanula lactiflora*, is another predictable wind casualty in my garden. At The Garden House, half of each bellflower clump is cut down to 2ft/60cm in late May; this creates stockier, self-supporting plants, and extends the blooming season. Known as the 'Chelsea chop' (since the job coincides with Chelsea Flower Show), this technique can be applied to many other tall perennials, including *Helenium*, *Rudbeckia* and *Helianthus*.

RESPECTABILITY FROM FOLIAGE

In Edwardian times, people had borders, even whole gardens, devoted to specific seasons, which you could avoid going into when there was nothing in flower. In today's plots, everything is permanently on view, so you have to keep the interest going. Leaves, stems and shapes are the principal means, since they are around a lot longer than flowers and fruits. So, whatever type of border you are making, I think it is sensible to make it as much of a sculpture as possible, with plenty of complementary textures and forms.

For me, that involves weaving foliage contrast into plantings I am otherwise assembling for their flower power, but you can simplify things by forgetting about flowers altogether. A foliage garden is one of the easiest styles to get right, and it is no coincidence that it is the favourite formula of the TV makeover programmes. Buy the likes of bamboos, phormiums, tree ferns, palms, grasses and cordylines from the garden centre, and you can immediately

← Like all tall delphiniums, my favourite 'Alice Artindale' (*top*) needs staking. At least it is reliably perennial. With most lilies, you never quite know – but they make stylish annuals: this is 'Citronella' (*bottom*).

see what they look like, what shapes complement each other, and where they are going to look good. Add a tree with a bold trunk as a year-round focal point, and the scene is complete.

The TV gardeners tend to use a fairly repetitive range of plants, because they want their borders to look punchy, and there are a limited number of visually exciting, yet hardy-ish, foliage plants available, especially in large sizes.

In fact, there are endless variations you can play on the leafy theme. At The Dingle, near Welshpool, Barbara Joseph has planted a predominantly grey-leaved border on a sunny bank, which is one of the best I have seen. Several plants of sea buckthorn, *Hippophae rhamnoides*, occupy the back row, giving a blur of silver above dark angular trunks. In front of them are dense grey mounds of Jerusalem sage, *Phlomis fruticosa*, and *Brachyglottis (Senecio)* 'Sunshine'. Then comes a beautiful scheme of alternating shrubs of green-flowered, blue-leaved *Euphorbia characias* and maroon-leaved *Berberis thunbergii* f. *atropurpurea*. And finally, lapping the lawn in the front row, are purple-leaved sage, silver cotton lavender, and grey catmint. Her garden is attached to the family nursery, which is very handy. 'I'm like a child living over a sweet shop,' she says.

MANAGING THE SEASONS

Orchestrating waves of flowering plants is a greater challenge (but with greater rewards), for there is a continual evolution through the seasons. Not only do individual plants come and go, but there are also more general changes, as shrubs and bulbs give way to a rising and then ebbing tide of summer perennials, each phase bringing its own dominant colours, shapes, heights and other qualities.

My recommendation is to simplify all this, by giving each section of border a peak flowering period, grouping a few different plants together that bloom simultaneously. Visually, I think this is much more satisfactory than spreading your flowers thinly, trying to give the impression the whole garden is alight.

→ The flowering season for shady areas is naturally early, but with a tapestry of leaf shapes and colours you can hold some interest right through the summer. This is my east-facing border: you can't get to the spider's web seat; it is purely an eye-catcher.

Instead, you will get a succession of proper climaxes, or honeypots, of blended colours. From a maintenance stance, this also has its benefits, for instead of scrutinizing the whole garden, the eye is directed to certain spots, and these are where you can concentrate your grooming and deadheading. In between the honeypots, structural plantings and foliage patterns hold the fort.

What size and shape you make these seasonal pictures depends on the size and layout of your garden, but they should be at least a generous eyeful. And if you can fit several or more of them into each view, so much the better. These might be at intervals along a straight line or, less formally, as a zig-zag within a border or across the width of the garden. You can expect several weeks' display from each picture, though by interplanting with bulbs, annuals or even climbing plants you can usually engineer a second flush of colour in the same spot.

In shady areas, the main flowering season is likely to be between February and June, when most woodlanders – shrubs, bulbs and perennials – are in bloom. During this time you can programme a number of colour changes, with attention shifting in slow succession from one part of the border to another. Here and there a prominent space ought to be reserved for a late event, like hydrangeas, Japanese anemones or a flaring maple.

In sunny areas, perennials don't really start getting into their stride until May, though bulbs and tree and shrub blossom can create sizeable early pools of colour. The season then goes from strength to strength, with crescendos every month until October, when it is back to bulbs and leaf tints.

4 — THE ART OF PLANTING

Ask half a dozen people to plant a border with the same palette of plants, and you will get half a dozen different pictures. I remember, years ago, helping a friend with her first gardening venture, planting out some trays of white alyssum and blue lobelia. We started off working back to back, and when I turned round, I found that she had been planting hers in alternate blue and white stripes, while I had been planting in monochrome drifts. She preferred her way.

Out and about, when you meet a really good piece of planting, it is always worth noting not only what plants are used, but how they are arranged, how big the clumps are, and which colour and shape is dominant. Often that means lifting your eyes to take in the surrounding influences. For example, focus only on the ground-level concentrations of fiery reds, oranges and yellows in Sissinghurst's Cottage Garden, and you miss the contribution of the enormous curtain of blush-white 'Madame Alfred Carrière', the climbing rose on the house wall, which gives bright and uplifting backlighting to what would otherwise be a garden of quite heavy tones.

SCALE

The scale of your planting – the size of each plant and each clump – is obviously going to change quite a bit within a garden. I suppose the general rule is that things should be in proportion: the bigger the setting, and the greater the distance at which the planting is seen, the more substantial the

← Previous page: A bold, foreground shape helps to give drama and perspective to a view. Here, *Phormium tenax* – which grows in bogs in New Zealand – frames the otherwise laid-back setting of my frog pond.

← Left: Instead of being segregated in distinct clumps, perennials like salvia, geranium and achillea are here merged in a border to give a meadowlike impression.

plants and clumps ought to be. There is probably an equation for it. James van Sweden, who designs against lakes, forests and the gigantic edifices of downtown Washington DC, often installs a hundred or more plants to each clump. He reckons you can still read his borders driving at 30 m.p.h.

In small spaces, overscaling can be entertaining. David Hicks was a master of it: a palace-sized painting in a rectory sitting-room, or a towering statue in a little courtyard. In a narrow passage at Butterstream, Jim Reynolds's garden in Trim, Ireland, you are forced to squeeze between box hedges that must be three times as wide as they ought to be. Dieticians would call them morbidly overweight: I call them cuddly.

But at the very least, a garden needs plants of sufficient height and bulk to make a visual link with house and surroundings. That means trees and large shrubs. In turn, these help bring the scale down, so that in the spaces in between, drifts of smaller shrubs, clumps of perennials, and even mats of alpines don't seem odd.

Vita Sackville-West wrote that it was an axiom of gardening that three plants of the same kind look better planted side by side than dotted about. It all depends on the look you want. I am thinking of Christopher Holliday's border at Grange-over-Sands, Cumbria, in which yellow-variegated phormiums are repeated as tufts through cushions of white, purple-backed, daisy-flowered osteospermums. Sure, one big drift of phormium behind one big drift of

osteospermum would look stunning, too, but it would also look rather more formal. Nature likes to mingle.

For me, it is about striking a balance between apparent spontaneity and the need for a design order. In practice, that means having a foundation of plants in readable blocks, Sackville-West style – each perennial in a generous clump, and the occasional shrub planted as a threesome – but here and there having the odd sparky solo act, perhaps a plant self-seeding, and occasionally having the border break down into mingled meadowy passages, along the lines of those at Lady Farm.

Whatever the style of planting, a good formula is to have dominance in every scene: one dominant mass, one dominant shape, and one dominant colour.

SHAPE, HEIGHT AND TEXTURE

The test of a good piece of planting, I was once told, is whether it photographs well in black and white. The message was that scenes hang as much on their blend of shapes and textures as on their colours – in fact, often more so, since for long stretches of time there is little colour present beyond the muted shades of branches and leaves.

It is a sound principle to work by, as long as it doesn't lead you into trying to exact maximum contrast from every single square foot of ground. Over some passages of border, it is nice to have planting that is quite soft, restful and uniform in its height and form.

I remember a beautiful scene in the Otari Native Plant Garden in Wellington, New Zealand, comprising rounded hummocks of carex and flowerless pampas grasses, backed by various hebes and hebe-like species. In a black and white photo, that would look a blur. In real life there was plenty of definition to it, because half the plants had leaves coloured copper or old gold – one of the quirks of NZ flora.

But generally, sculptural contrasts between neighbouring plants make for a more interesting composition. Differences in height, for instance. Think of the

← The kaleidoscope of perennials in the Cretan garden at The Garden House allows the eye to float across to the church tower beyond. There are no strong shapes or colour blocks to disrupt the misty view.

dull amorphous lump of a mixed municipal shrubbery, where even if individual plants want to be taller than their companions they are soon pruned into submission. How much livelier it would be if the planting undulated in waves, front to back and side to side, with the odd well-spaced big structure erupting among them.

Planting should rise, fall and meander 'like the flight of a butterfly'. This is how Marnie Hall, the gardener naturalist, put it to me years ago, and it is a poetic image that has stuck.

I did once have a meeting with my local councillors to put them straight on this and many other urban planting matters, but I think they thought I was a bit mad. My butterfly impression was probably a mistake.

Here and there, quite big plunges in height are worth engineering, particularly where strong vertical shapes are involved, which take on much more importance when there is empty space around them. For example, at Edinburgh Botanic Garden there is a stunning planting of coloured yuccas, phormiums and pampas grasses all set in ground-hugging mats of pink-flowered diascia and blue-leaved acaena. And at Wakehurst Place, Sussex, several widely-spaced clumps of white-stemmed bramble (*Rubus*) leap out of waves of heathers, like the white horses in that famous advert.

This idea can be carried into the bigger scale, too, as at The Garden House, where shrubbery suddenly drops on to the flat planes of lawn, gravel and a sculpted slope of prostrate thymes, before rising again into herbaceous borders and woods.

Vertical shapes contrast particularly well with the general run of vaguely rounded vegetation, and can be used as a motif through a planting – thin, erect *Iris sibirica* leaves weaving through a waterside scheme of feathery astilbes, say.

In one of the huge summer borders at Butterstream, Ireland, repeated clumps of blue delphiniums spear through swathes of violet *Campanula lactiflora*, *Achillea ptarmica* 'The Pearl' and silver-leaved *Artemisia ludoviciana*, with short white verbascum spikes and specks of pink phlox in between. Further along, all this merges into an ocean of vertical white rosebay willowherb

(*Epilobium angustifolium* var. *album*), pink foxgloves and mauve thalictrum. A masterly scene.

I use foxgloves as punctuation in my own little orchard garden, among the billowy shapes of shrub roses, hardy geraniums, *Viola cornuta* and the like. But since they seldom sow themselves where I want them, I have to do a fair amount of lifting and repositioning. Often I do this as late as early June, when naturally they are taken by surprise, but I help them along by reducing their burden of leaves and watering copiously. The previous autumn would be a better time to move them, but I forget.

Of course, as well as contrast in height and shape, flowers and leaves can also contrast potently in size (box next to bergenia, yucca next to santolina, rose next to catmint) and texture, with some reflecting light and some absorbing it: glossy against matt (*Viburnum davidii* with yew), smooth against hairy (acanthus with alchemilla), fleshy against coarse (*Sedum* 'Herbstfreude' with *Artemisia pontica*). All this adds to the interest of a planting.

↑ A low carpet of thymes creates a variation in height amid shrubs and perennials at The Garden House.

COLOUR SCHEMING

There aren't any rules in colour scheming. Almost every combination of colours works at an individual level, but you have to stand back and consider the big picture. If each colour is just a dot, as in Keith Wiley's Cretan meadow at The Garden House, everything merges into a jolly kaleidoscope. But if you plant in clumps you start reading each colour separately, and without order and pattern the picture doesn't make sense. Colour influences the mood of a garden as much as it does a room in the house. Organize your colours, and you can differentiate between scenes, spring ambushes, direct the eye where you want it to go, and produce the right reactions.

The flavour of each colour comes across most potently when you isolate it. This is triumphantly apparent in the Dublin garden of writer Helen Dillon, dubbed the best gardener in Ireland. She has divided up her one-acre plot into a sweltering, red-flowered, purple-leaved border; a chirpy yellow garden; a calming blue and violet border; a green sorbet garden; a romantic mix of silvers and pastels . . .

It is perfection, but hard-earned. Helen is out there dawn to dusk, tweaking, polishing, and moving things around until she finds just the right spot. 'Piss off. I'm busy,' hangs the sign on the potting shed. The place is packed with rarities, and I always walk around drooling.

Single colour plantings like this are obviously high art, but if there aren't too many ingredients, you can achieve a natural look. In a park in Ensköping, Sweden, Piet Oudolf has planted an enormous belt of several colour forms of hardy purple salvia (S. × *sylvestris* 'Blauhügel', S. × s. 'Rügen', and S. *nemorosa* 'Ostfriesland') which has all the sumptuous quality of a heather moor. In all colour schemes, as much interest comes from the interplay of tones, pale and deep, as from different colour hues.

Here and there, you can keep to monocolour incidents – a trio of *Verbena bonariensis*, *Dahlia merckii* and *Thalictrum delavayi*, say, which gives you an elegant blend of lilac and a sophisticated contrast of shapes.

Generally, though, I think more fun is to be had from mixing colours. The tried and tested recipe is to divide the so-called cool colours (silver, white, pink, violet, blue, blue-green) from the hot colours (lime-green, yellow, orange, red, purple), and keep the two groups apart, with muted greens and greys acting as a bridge between them. I like to insert at least a crack of contrast to wake things up – lemon or lime among the cool colours; violet or white among the hot colours – but otherwise this is an appealing formula.

Here are some of my favourite harmonies, which I shall flesh out in later chapters: (hot) orange, yellow and lime-green; scarlet and salmon; scarlet and purple; (cool) white, lemon and grey; blue, grey and white; violet, magenta, crimson and silver; pink, crimson, violet-blue and white.

Cool colours tend to seem further away than they are, so they make good background tints, to give a sense of depth to a border and a garden. In Sussex, artist Elizabeth Woodhouse plants one of her borders literally as a sky, with swirling silvery elaeagnus leaves representing cloud, and holes punched through to reveal azure specks of delphinium behind. She was inspired by Tiepolo. (It contrasts with a rich, dark, warm Rubens border, and a scheme of white rambler rose, apricot-flowered perennials and bronze carex sedges – the best use of carex I have seen; often, it simply looks dead.)

Cool and pale colours can look rather washed out in full sun, but with the softer light of the evening they come into their own. White is then the brightest beacon. By contrast, the hot and dark colours grab the attention by day, scarlet and brilliant yellow the prime targets.

But it is daft to stick to safe harmonies and deprive yourself of half the possible colour effects. Mixtures of hot and cool colours, though usually stimulating, don't have to be as startling as a black and white cottage. Alter the intensity of the opponents – plum tulips and grey cardoon leaves, say – and you get a quieter contrast.

Here are some of my favourite contrasts: blue and yellow; white and gold; violet, yellow and lime-green; scarlet and white; scarlet, violet and lime-green; red and blue; lemon, orange and glaucous blue; scarlet, orange, yellow and grey.

To pull all this together in a garden scene, I tend to think in terms of extrovert colours and mild-mannered colours. Extroverts include the strong yellows, scarlets and flower-packed whites, and saturated shockers like orange 'Enchantment' lilies and magenta-pink Japanese azaleas (the azaleas used wonderfully eccentrically at Sheffield Park, Sussex, tight-clipped in the grass like a flock of pink sheep). Wherever they are, whether in harmonious or contrasting company, they are going to draw the eye. So you need either to isolate them – say in the centre of a border – or use them sparingly, as a bit of snap, crackle and pop amid the flow of gentler shades. Unless you are going for all-out cabaret – 'shocking beauty' Tom Hobbs calls it.

Dominant repeating colours help to unify all the disparate bits. A dreamy example is the meadow of summer annuals planted by Tim Rees in France. From a distance, all you see is a haze of white – from *Ammi majus*, a refined cousin of cow parsley. But once among it, you find yourself in a jewel box sparkling with specks of scarlet, orange, magenta, yellow and purple in any number of colour combinations.

Finally, there is the matter of taste. I can't understand Piet Oudolf's predilection for sombre schemes of browns, mauves and crimson reds. And to me, the mauve and yellow mixtures in the gravel garden in Munich's Westpark are downright repulsive. Maybe it's to do with nationality – national colour preferences are well known to advertisers. Also, did you know that the eye sees colour differently as it ages, so that an older person's harmony may be a younger person's clash? This explains a lot, I tell Christopher Lloyd, the master clasher.

RHYTHM PLANTING

The best way of knitting a piece of planting together, and giving it a strong identity, is to repeat some of the ingredients. This is what you see in nature, and it is the foundation for artful gardening, too.

In the formal herbaceous border, it is traditional to set out clumps of the

→ Repeated stands of *Kniphofia* 'Atlanta' and *Iris* 'Butterscotch Kiss' set the early summer mood of the gravel or 'steppe' garden at Lady Farm. They grow out of a matrix of *Achillea* 'Moonshine', eryngium, coreopsis and tuft-forming grasses.

same plant at more or less equal intervals down its length. For example, at Snowshill Manor, near Broadway, purple sage alternates with green alchemilla along the front of the narrow main bed, with oriental poppies, foxgloves, geraniums and day-lilies repeated down the middle row. Plenty of other shrubs and perennials appear as single clumps and lone drifts, but there is enough repetition for the eye to perceive a coherent idea.

Charles Wade, who set out the garden in the 1920s, believed in a garden having a strong architectural plan. But he was otherwise a great eccentric, packing his house so full of curiosities (Japanese armour, model boats, doll's houses, policeman's truncheons, you name it) that he had to move out and live in a nearby cottage. Queen Mary, visiting in 1937, said he was the most notable part of the whole collection.

In a more relaxed style of garden, the repetitions will be more abstract. Within Beth Chatto's meandering gravel garden, various rhythm plants are discernible. Some, like ornamental grasses and sedums, may be confined to one bed. Others, like bergenias and euphorbias, repeat through the entire garden. Euphorbias are particularly rewarding rhythm plants because there are so many slightly different species with the same curious flower structure and lime-green tints, which allows you to play variations on your theme.

Their milky sap is a hazard, though. I have been in Casualty myself with burning eyes. I had been removing their spent flower stems in the morning, and around teatime, several hand-washes later, I rubbed my eyes. Some years before, I had talked about the sap on *Gardeners' World*, breaking a stem with my bare hands, and I remembered the panic back in the studio at the prospect of all those remonstrating viewers' letters. So our late anchorman Geoff Hamilton was roped in to substitute his gloved hands, which were then pasted into the film. I thought this was a bit excessive at the time. Now I know better, and always wear my Marigolds and goggles.

You can use anything as a rhythm plant, though obviously you get a longer contribution from foliage, and from flowers that develop slowly and have good seedheads. Whether you use something bold, like spiky blue delphiniums or globular white *Hydrangea arborescens* 'Annabelle', or misty, like repeating waves of lavender or forget-me-nots, or indeed a combination of all these, depends on the look you want. I would scan the list of plants that you are keen to grow in each bed, and select a few favourites, with the right season, colour, height, shape and personality.

Having a few plants reappear through a bed is one thing, but you can go further, by constructing the border around a company of plants which are repeated as a unit. Again, this can be done in a formal or an abstract way, but it does simplify the planting process considerably.

At Coleton Fishacre, on the south Devon coast – the former home of the D'Oyly Carte family (and no doubt their sisters and their cousins and their aunts) – there is a memorable repeating shrubby pattern of trailing rosemaries, grey-leaved helianthemums, green hebes, and blue-flowered *Lithodora diffusa* on the sunny terraced beds below the house. All that contrasting foliage would look good most of the year.

A purely herbaceous scheme, on the other hand, may hold together for quite a short time, as in the stony mountain meadow garden at Weihenstephan University, in Freising, near Munich. Here, the ground is covered in a low silver and grey tapestry of repeating catmint, salvias and *Stachys byzantina*, through which sprout recurring tufts of cream dropwort (*Filipendula vulgaris*

'Multiplex'), *Euphorbia griffithii* 'Fireglow', and orange 'Fire King' lilies. It was the first piece of new wave German planting I ever saw, and I was poleaxed.

In the smaller scale of his Hertfordshire border, Tom Stuart-Smith repeats swags of the magenta geraniums *G. psilostemon* and *G.* 'Ann Folkard', hardy purple salvias, and lime-yellow *Euphorbia ceratocarpa*. In turn, these are spiked by the repeated verticals of verbascums, mauve *Allium hollandicum*, mauve-white *Salvia sclarea* var. *turkestanica* (sweaty armpit smell, but certainly a looker), and the grass *Calamagrostis* × *acutiflora* 'Karl Foerster'.

Cleverly, the colour scheme echoes the tints of the wild purple knapweed and yellow bird's-foot trefoil in the meadow beyond, while the calamagrostis echoes the native grasses. But the present harmony and simplicity of the border is the result of Tom allowing it to evolve over the years, with the plants happiest on his soil eventually taking over. There are no thugs present, so diversity has been preserved.

This is an exemplary way of naturalistic gardening: watching what nature is up to, letting things seed and move around, and simply editing, arresting and amending as necessary.

MATRIX PLANTS

In the wild, there is often one dominant type of plant through which everything else is growing – grasses or buttercups in a meadow, say, and ferns or bluebells in a wood. This is another way of approaching rhythmic planting.

At the Westpark in Munich, various short, slim ornamental grasses are set

↑ | *Euphorbia polychroma* is a lively contributor for many weeks in spring.

out as a matrix over the gravelly soil, into which all the colourful perennials, like bearded irises, yellow asphodels, sedums and mountain asters, are inserted. As in a meadow, you look across a sea of plants all of much the same height. But the grasses are clump-forming, and often spaced several feet apart, so this isn't a dense, integrated sward.

At Lady Farm, the mid-height grass *Calamagrostis × acutiflora* 'Karl Foerster' is used as a matrix down the 'prairie' slope. Between its tufts are drifts of late summer daisies, notably copper-orange *Helenium* 'Moerheim Beauty' and yellow rudbeckias – their horizontal layers of flower contrasting nicely with the grass's upright stems.

But there are many plants you can use as a matrix. I think the hazier sorts have particular appeal because they highlight all other shapes. In the tiny paved garden in front of artist John Hubbard's house at Chilcombe, Dorset, *Astrantia major* and *Alchemilla mollis* have been allowed to spread through all the cracks, creating a grey-white and lime-yellow backdrop for the magenta pelargoniums and other bright exotics in the terracotta pots between them. This is one of the most brilliantly colour-schemed gardens I have seen. On my first visit, even his ginger Cairn terrier was posing in just the right spot, in front of a wall of white rambler rose, fringed in fiery phygelius.

In his garden at Ruinen, Holland, Ton ter Linden let *Geranium pyrenaicum* seed right through a border, front to back, and side to side. Its tiny lilac flowers, produced in clouds through the summer, were the speckled backdrop to gorgeous orange and salmon oriental poppies, mauve and purple *Allium hollandicum*, blue geraniums, and pink and wine-black columbines, all of which were dotted through the border in carefree style. The effect was like an Impressionist painting.

Lilac *Verbena bonariensis* is, with fennel, one of the best tall matrix plants, because it is so skeletal and flowers for so long. It is much used in contemporary French bedding schemes, as a partner for flamboyant annuals. I have admired it in this role at the annual summer-long garden festival at Chaumont, on the Loire. This is well worth a visit. Plenty of nonsense is guaranteed (a bench fitted with water-jets to soak your guests, for example, or a garden paved with bones

– a special challenge for visitors who had brought their dogs and, on the day I went, distinctly whiffy). But there are sure to be plenty of inspiring ideas, too, such as a glass dining-table with built-in herb garden, or a pond with floating seats.

In one show garden the verbena was blended with another fine matrix plant, *Calamintha nepeta* – also long-blooming, with a haze of tiny flowers in palest lilac on short, upright stems. Startling orange crocosmias were dotted through. Artists call this the 'zing' effect.

My landscape architect friend Brita von Schoenaich uses the white cow-parsley-like annual *Ammi majus* as a long-lasting matrix plant in a summer border for clients in Essex. Waves of colour from other annuals – opium poppies, violet-blue phacelia, pink and white cosmos, blue cornflowers, violet echiums, pink clary and red flax – ripple through it, and it fair hums with insect life.

In effect this is a bedding scheme, but one that is sown direct on to the soil in spring, rather than planted out – an idea that has great labour-saving potential for the home gardener, and introduces a wonderful pastoral feel.

5 — THE BIG PICTURE

The bleakest weeks of midwinter are the best time to consider the framework of a garden, when your thoughts are less likely to be derailed by all those perennials. Coloured hay, the garden designer Russell Page called them, which makes the point. You can't structure a garden with hay. Top priority must be the larger shapes and masses, deciduous and evergreen, which will give the garden its year-round substance, compose views, and help create the different subdivisions.

DESIGNING WITH TREES

I used to think of trees as background objects, but I was put straight on my first visit to the east coast of America. There, many houses are built in the forest, often inches away from great oaks and maples (where the soil isn't shrinkable clay, root damage isn't usually much of a worry). So the views out of the windows are through a tracery of branches, which half-conceals the garden beyond. As in photography, this gives framing and perspective, and adds a bit of mystery; similarly, it is rather nice looking back at a house through the arch of a tree.

Immediately on my return home, I installed a paperbark maple, *Acer griseum*, in the main border 20ft/6m away from the house wall, smack bang in front of the sitting-room window. The prize quality of this small tree, apart from its light, elegant canopy of leaves which turns red in late October, is its perpetually flaking copper-brown bark. When backlit by the sun, especially on

← Previous page: A strong bone structure is evident around the house at The Garden House, where a combination of clipped shapes, natural forms and architectural detail ensures year-round entertainment.

← Left: Paperbark maple, *Acer griseum*, warms your cockles even in the depth of winter. It is a good tree for small gardens.

a winter's day, it looks as if it is being licked by flames – so don't plant it on your north boundary, where you can't get behind it. Generally, deciduous trees are better backlit; evergreens lit from the front.

At Bodnant, North Wales, paperbark maple is memorably silhouetted against an inferno of orange azaleas, one of the appetizers for the rhododendron spectacle that fills the valley below. I once asked Lord Aberconway if he had ever been to the Himalayas. 'No,' he replied. 'There has never seemed much point.'

Trees take on a sculptural importance when they are free-standing, inside the garden. So a fleeting show of flowers is not enough. They have to have year-round presence. Some trees, like crab-apples, achieve this with a succession of events – spring blossom, summer poise, autumn tints and early winter fruits. Others achieve it with a charismatic outline, like an old mulberry or a cut-leaf sumach, *Rhus typhina* 'Dissecta', whose antlers stand proud in the centre of my main border; or the front garden magnolia, *M.* × *soulangeana*, whose low spreading structure presides over many a grass glade and terrace (anywhere that it won't be disturbed; it cannot tolerate digging); 'Lennei Alba' and rose-pink 'Rustica Rubra' are good cultivars.

Secateurs and pruning saw can be wielded to improve a tree's outline, lifting the leaf canopy and thinning interior branches. A few minutes' work can transform a scene, though you have to proceed slowly and constantly assess your handiwork. Branches don't glue back very well.

Bark is a very good reason for choosing a tree, and birches as well as maples are prime contenders. The whiter than white *Betula utilis* var. *jacquemontii* is too crude for me, and in any case, with the blue paint and the 'water feature', is now becoming an embarrassing cliché. There are a number of subtler barks. My own favourites are the copper, pink and grey of Chinese *B. albosinensis* var. *septentrionalis*, and the deep craggy brown of the American river birch, *B. nigra* 'Heritage' (it loves damp ground, but this is not essential).

Both star in the birch glade at Kalmthout Arboretum, Belgium, developed by the late Robert de Belder and his wife Jelena, one of the most inspiring and poetic gardeners I have ever met. I am putty in her hands as she discusses the merits of Fuji cherries, *Prunus incisa*, giving 'the first great bee concert of spring'; or as she wonders aloud why there aren't radio announcements telling people where to go to see the bluebells and 'the dance of the young beech leaves'.

Her birches are set in a wood of larger trees and arranged in a wide zig-zag, backed by evergreen shrubs (rhododendrons, if I recall) and all wrapping around a central lung of lawn. It would be an excellent blueprint for a town garden. Several of her birches also sport more than one trunk, which adds to their impact. In nature, trees are not always presented as neat solo acts, with one clean, straight stem. Similarly, in gardens it is sometimes nice to plant a stand of two or three trees very close together (even in the same hole) or to select a tree that branches low to the ground.

With birches, which regenerate well, you can achieve the multi-stemmed effect by cutting your tree to the ground after a couple of years. Keith Wiley did this with his trio of cream-trunked birches, *Betula ermanii* 'Grayswood Hill', at The Garden House, though I gather he said a small prayer at the time; the trees

↑ *Betula ermanii* 'Grayswood Hill' displays its multi-stemmed habit after surgery at The Garden House.

had been expensive. For a small woodland tree with patterned bark, *Stewartia pseudocamellia* takes some beating. White flowers in summer and rich autumn tints give it all-round appeal, but it must have acid soil.

ECCENTRIC TREES

I have mixed thoughts about trees with eccentrically coloured leaves. At Kerdalo, Prince Wolkonsky planted an entire strip of hillside with golden trees and shrubs to combat the grey Brittany skies. That took some nerve. On the one hand, coloured trees are a disruptive presence if you are trying to create a tranquil, natural mood. After all, Britain is supposed to be green and pleasant, not zany like a cartoon. On the other hand, the golds do warm your cockles, and the purples introduce sumptuous shadow at the end of a vista.

The principle I follow is at least to keep the garden backdrop to greens and greys. I can't do much about the two huge copper beeches I inherited on my western boundary. I wouldn't have chosen them, but have come to revere them, especially in early summer when I open my bedroom curtains on to an ocean of terracotta. Otherwise, if I feel the need for a dose of coloured leaves, I pick from among plants that aren't going to rise into the skyline – large shrubs like purple hazel or smoke bush (*Cotinus*), or small trees like the yellow hop tree, *Ptelea trifoliata* 'Aurea', which I grow in a north-facing bed,

spiked by white foxgloves. Its limy flowers have a scent as heady as an April viburnum.

In surroundings of typically rounded trees, a vertical tree makes a strong eyecatcher – none more powerful than a dark conifer. In gardens, they are often used either as a sentinel to draw your eye to a building or as a boundary marker to terminate a view. In this role, the most dramatic I know is the Lombardy poplar at Chirk Castle, near Oswestry. Standing at the end of a long lawn and border vista, it is silhouetted almost head to toe against the sky, for the ground falls away steeply into a panorama said to encompass fourteen counties. (Remember to bring a pinch of salt.)

For the average garden, the upright pear, *Pyrus calleryana* 'Chanticleer', is a better alternative, fast-growing and handsome in leaf and blossom. And where there is room for its eventually wide, bulbous shape, I recommend the hornbeam, *Carpinus betulus* 'Fastigiata'. Drivers of the Oxford ring road will have noticed what a fine avenue tree it makes. The rush-hour pace is ideal for admiring them. Not everyone shares my view. 'This is one of my least favourite plants,' the garden writer and botanical editor Tony Lord wrote to me. 'Just a blob on a stick.'

BACKDROP TREES

You don't have to be so demanding of backdrop trees, which are not under daily scrutiny. Indeed, often their most important role is not as ornament but to screen away an eyesore or hide you from the neighbours. A few thoughts. A small tree in the foreground is as effective a block as a large tree further away. You also get a more natural picture if you stagger your blocking trees and evergreens over the full depth of a garden, rather than leaving everything to a dense line on the boundary.

Then there is the option, albeit a pricey one, of buying big. Gardeners have been transplanting hefty trees for centuries; I know of trees moved in Connecticut with attached rootballs of a quarter of an acre – done with the aid

← Slow-growing and seldom seen, the yellow hop tree, *Ptelea trifoliata* 'Aurea', is a top contender for bringing a limy glow to shady borders.

of a missile transporter. I am not suggesting this; in any case, your average tool-hire shop doesn't offer missile transporters. But instead of planting something fast-growing, which may keep on growing long past your optimum height, you can install a semi-mature tree that is already large, but never going to be enormous.

On the other hand, it is a mistake to think that small space always means small tree. The scale of a house or urban panorama often cries out for an enormous green counterweight.

THEME TREES

It is a tantalizing business wandering around an arboretum, trying to narrow your choice to just one or two trees for your own pocket-handkerchief of a plot. But at the same time, there is invariably a lesson staring you in the face: as models of design, most arboreta are complete dog's dinners, compared to the satisfying rhythms of a wood, orchard or willowy riverbank. All that variety of height, shape, colour and character is indigestible. Themes, and variations on themes, are the key to good tree planting – indeed, all planting.

So, back home, the choice is to echo or contrast with the trees around you. If there is already a strong established theme in the neighbourhood, then it's carte blanche for an exciting contrast – the wide, low, big-leaved dome of an Indian bean tree (*Catalpa*) set against all the dark, conifer columns, say, or the picturesque eruption of a pine among the street's cherries. I love pines and cherries together, especially those cherries that bloom on bare branches, like the white winter cherry, *Prunus × subhirtella* 'Autumnalis', and the pale pink, almond-scented Yoshino cherry, *P. × yedoensis*, which flowers in March.

But even if you are playing a contrast, you want a tree that has some link with the vegetation around it. A eucalyptus popping up among apple trees or Japanese maples, for instance, is very odd, though it is becoming a common sight in many towns.

→ *Crataegus laevigata* 'Paul's Scarlet' packs quite a punch in May.

To stoke up a cottagey or pastoral mood, the obvious ornamental trees to turn to are those related to our native hedgerow and orchard species, like thorns, pears, crab-apples and cherries. Like their country counterparts, they look right standing alone or widely spaced, in borders or grass.

The red-flowered version of Midland hawthorn, *Crataegus laevigata* 'Paul's Scarlet', is a prime contender. I once saw it in Ireland, knee-deep in cow parsley, and it looked a picture, but it combines well with more sophisticated company. One garden, near New College, Oxford, has a Chinese wisteria threaded through it, so arresting a sight that I narrowly missed a pedestrian on my Honda motorcycle. The crab, *Malus hupehensis*, is a more elegant all-rounder, with white blossom and red fruits, and in its moment of glory, the foaming whites and pinks of *M. floribunda* are quite knockout.

Other fine forms are *Crataegus persimilis* 'Prunifolia', with fiery autumn colour and red fruits, and *C. × lavallei* 'Carrierei', which makes a dense

umbrella-head of glossy leaves. And there is a wide choice of long-lasting fruits among the decorative *Malus* varieties, such as 'John Downie', 'Red Sentinel', and 'Golden Hornet'.

WILDERNESS TREES

Like birches, pines and many other conifers, rowans suggest rugged, upland country, and so are good trees for standing alone among rocks, heathers and mountain meadow perennials – what German gardeners call 'steppe' planting.

I don't see any point growing an orange-berried rowan. In most parts of the country, the fruits are gobbled up by the blackbirds and thrushes even before they ripen. But birds are as suspicious of the pink and white-berried Asian rowans as I am of those brightly coloured cakes in Scottish tea shops. The pick of the pack is *Sorbus hupehensis*, particularly in its cultivar 'Pink Pagoda', which has blue-green feathery foliage and a usually heavy crop of pink and crimson pearls, often complemented by red autumn leaf colour.

S. vilmorinii has the drawback of June flowers that smell like a dead rat stuck in the drainpipe, but it is otherwise a lovely miniature tree with small leaves, deep red fruits, and red autumn colour. *S. cashmiriana* and *S. forrestii* are excellent whites, well partnered in Jimmy Hancock's Welsh garden by wild red fuchsia.

WOODLAND GLADE TREES

The woodland mood obviously relies on a community of trees growing fairly closely together. A dense, fairly tall boundary planting can be tiered down into an open glade, fringed in smaller trees and shrubs. More naturally, the odd trunk of a big tree will spear through the lower plants, so that every view is framed by columns. Deep-rooting oaks are the ideal framework trees, but there are many other smaller, faster options, such as wild cherry, *Prunus avium*.

Magnolias, maples, cherries and birches all blend happily. For a more natural mood, the more graceful, smaller-leaved *Magnolia × loebneri* hybrids are ideal. White 'Merrill' and pink 'Leonard Messel' are the best, wonderful on a frosty April day, against bare-branched trees and one of those crisp blue skies. *M. sieboldii* subsp. *sinensis* is one of several excellent short but spreading summer-flowering magnolias, with pendent scented white saucers.

The only downside with a magnolia is that it tends to be a one-season tree, which you may resent if you have to stare at it all year. Cherries are better, giving you a flash of orange in October (notably good in *Prunus sargentii*), or, in the case of *P. serrula*, a polished mahogany trunk (stunning on young trees). The winter cherry, *P. × subhirtella* 'Autumnalis', is in a class of its own, with good autumn tints and an inordinately long flowering season just when you need it, warding off many a phone-call to the Samaritans.

Several times I have been lucky enough to be in New York State in October, when the forested hillsides were ablaze. I remember a particularly fine view from the army football stadium at West Point; the game was unintelligible, but whenever a goal was scored, cannons fired and cadets cantered along the touchline on mules, with swords drawn. Because of our lack of sunshine – which is what helps leaves manufacture plenty of colour-enhancing sugars –

↑ Spring and autumn see the serious action in woodland borders. *Magnolia × loebneri* 'Merrill' (*left*) peaks very early; *Liquidambar styraciflua* 'Lane Roberts' (*right*) very late.

many of these American trees perform disappointingly in Britain, none more so than sugar maple, a principal constituent of the blaze. But there are exceptions. A selected form of red maple, like *Acer rubrum* 'Schlesingeri' or *A. r.* 'October Glory', and tulip tree, *Liriodendron tulipifera*, which turns butter-yellow, certainly earn their keep in the larger garden.

And for the average garden there is sweet gum, *Liquidambar styraciflua*, in a cultivar like 'Lane Roberts' or 'Worplesdon'. A solitary specimen commanding a pool of lawn is a prize feature, as it is in the centre of my local London square (the only decent plant in it). The rainbow tints appear on its fingered leaves often as late as mid-November, and in youth it has a compact, columnar shape.

Given protection from cold wind and hot midday sun, and soil that is not too dry, a company of Japanese maples makes a fine theme for a glade. And, if necessary, they will squeeze into a very small space, since many are shrub-sized. The Holford family used to host October parties in their maple glades at Westonbirt Arboretum, Gloucestershire. Rich Edwardians had life sorted out. Of the taller, 20ft/6m maples, *Acer palmatum* 'Osakazuki' and *A. japonicum* 'Vitifolium' turn a dazzling scarlet, especially potent when backlit.

Another small, shade-happy tree is *Amelanchier lamarckii*. I rate it highly, but since it is so easy-going, it is much misused by local councils, who condemn it to collecting litter and syringes in dingy shrubberies. I have several multi-stemmed stands of it, one of them under the skirt of a big beech, where it gets very little direct sun. And yet the white spring blossom and red autumn tints are reliable.

DRY GARDEN TREES

To help foster an Italian mood at Hidcote, Major Johnston made much use of the evergreen holm oak, *Quercus ilex*, as a theme tree. This dark, cloud-like oak, though slow-growing, is ultimately huge, but when it outgrows its welcome you can lop it back to its trunk and it will re-sprout (like planes and limes). Alternatively, you can clip it back annually to a compact dome.

In smaller gardens, eucalyptus are a little easier to live with as mature trees because they are slimmer and cast less shade. I have a twelve-year-old enormously tall Tingiringi gum, *E. glaucescens*, in my gravel garden, which is a great beauty, continually flaking off great green, grey and copper shards to reveal smooth, metallic, grey-white bark underneath. Unlike its cousins which race for the sky, snow gum, *E. paucifolia* subsp. *niphophila*, invariably leans sideways. The white tactile trunk, contoured like a horse's neck, demands a rub and a slap as you pass.

The main drawback with large evergreens is that they do create an expanse of dry soil around them, which is continually littered with falling leaves. You don't get this problem with wispy trees like Australian mimosa or pink Persian albizia, two exotics that are a serious option in London and the milder counties.

Nor with Mount Etna broom, *Genista aetnensis*, which makes a 15ft/5m waterfall of wiry branches, smothered in sweetly scented, brassy yellow pea-flowers in summer. It casts virtually no shade, but it is a little unstable and usually needs a supporting stake. Spookily, I was planting mine in Wales when an earthquake struck, of sufficient strength to rattle the windows. The epicentre was in our very town. I can show you fear in a handful of potting compost.

Judas tree, *Cercis siliquastrum*, sprouts mauve-pink flowers directly out of its bare branches. Plenty of heat helps it ward off coral spot disease, to which it is alarmingly susceptible. For grey leaves, I would go for a variant of our native chalkland whitebeam like *Sorbus aria* 'Lutescens' (disgusting flower scent), or the much overlooked snow pear, *Pyrus nivalis*, which gives the effect of silver willow on dry soil.

DAMP GARDEN TREES

It is willows and poplars that advertise the lakes and watercourses out in the countryside, but in gardens the questing roots of the large mature species are not compatible with houses. However, it is common practice to pollard, or prune back to a stump, coloured-stemmed forms of white willow, *Salix alba*, like orange *S. a.* subsp. *vitellina* 'Britzensis' and yellow *S. a.* subsp. *vitellina*, and this way they make a manageable thicket in the border – and a highlight of winter. Also, there are many willows of large shrub or small tree size, from the elegant maroon-twigged *S. purpurea* 'Nancy Saunders' to *S. babylonica* var. *pekinensis* 'Tortuosa' with wriggly branches.

Willows and poplars will accept fairly dry soil, too, which is handy, since you are often trying to create a watery mood on ground that isn't damp, such as around an artificial pond. Other large trees to call on here are the conical Italian alder, *Alnus cordata*, and Raywood ash, *Fraxinus angustifolia* 'Raywood', a willowy globe that turns purple in autumn.

But some trees do demand moist ground. *Cercidiphyllum japonicum* is usually encountered as an upright multi-stemmed tree, but there is a splendid weeping version, 'Pendulum', which makes a slimmer alternative to weeping willow for the garden pondside. Both have leaves opening a warm tan (well-partnered with creamy daffodils at Knightshayes, Devon) and departing in gold and, sometimes, pink. At this moment, its sugars release a delectable caramel scent, which persists in the dry leaves for a long time. Jelena de Belder had the idea of stuffing teddy bears with them. *Nyssa sylvatica* is the finest autumn-tinting waterside tree for acid soil.

INSTALLING TREES

Specialist nurseries offer plants bare-rooted or rootballed, delivered between autumn and spring, and this is a good way of buying a tree. They are usually decent-sized and better proportioned than the garden centre version. Most trees look somewhat shell-shocked for a year or two after planting, after which they should grow away strongly.

A young tree with a good head of branches needs staking. For many, this means lashing it to a tall pole, but we now know that swaying in the wind in-duces a tree to thicken. So the stake should be short, and the tree secured with an expandable tie and spacer, nailed to the stake to prevent rubbing and bashing.

Trees prefer square holes to round ones. I gleaned this bizarre bit of research from Tony Kirkham at Kew. In heavy soils especially, the young roots apparently find it much easier to break out into the surrounding ground via corners; given a curve, they are tempted to spiral. I hope somebody earned a doctorate for this little nugget.

CONIFERS

People are snooty about conifers, and they do have unfortunate associations with Mr Heath's 1970s, when a pall of idleness fell over the country and the zero-maintenance garden, complete with rugs of heathers and ground-cover, was everyone's dream.

Twenty-five years on, most of the dumpy dwarf conifers of rock gardens still leave me cold. Slow-growing is a better word than dwarf. I was once shown an old collection of them, among which there was hardly a tree under 30ft/9m. The bright yellow and blue conifers are also dangerously Disneyworld. But, as with all corners of the plant kingdom, once you start probing you uncover gems.

Pines must be not only the most picturesque but also the most atmospheric of all trees, evocative of both cold upland and warm coastal climates. At Kiftsgate, Gloucestershire, Scots and Monterey pines are theme trees, helping to stoke up a Mediterranean mood on the steep escarpment, and casting only patchy shade as the sun moves across the sky.

The stone pine, *Pinus pinea*, is the umbrella-shaped pine you see in tandem with slim cypresses on Italian hillsides. It is characterful alone or in a group, as my designer friend Tim Rees has used it in the South of France to cloak a small hill. His American clients commissioned him to build the hill, too, to screen an electricity pylon. It is amazing what you can do with a million dollars. This hardy pine would be my top choice for a gravel garden, closely followed by Mexican Montezuma pine, *P. montezumae*, which carries its feathery needles in cockade-like bunches.

For rocky or 'steppe' planting, I would go for damson-coned Korean fir, *Abies koreana*, or Bosnian pine, *P. heldreichii* (*P. leucodermis*), with rich green foliage and attractive young shoots in grey and tan. Its fairly compact, upright shape also recommends it as a boundary tree for the medium-sized garden, perhaps in combination with birches. To preside over an exotic Asian woodland glade, I would pick Japanese white pine, *P. parviflora*, the pine of willow-tree-pattern china, or, given enough room, Bhutan pine, *P. wallichiana*, a filigree beauty with blue-green needles.

EXCLAMATORY SHAPES

Otherwise, my taste in conifers is directed more towards the tighter, denser, more emphatic shapes. The taller, rocket-shaped species such as redwoods, Lawson cypress and western red cedar are, like pines, dramatic backdrop plants, for grouping behind the rounded outlines of deciduous trees. And, of course, they are hugely popular as visual screens – the fast-growing *Thuja*

↑ The tactile blue cones of my Korean fir, *Abies koreana*, have ambushed several friends into confronting their anti-conifer prejudices.

plicata 'Atrovirens' is the one I have used at home. They are particularly happy in the moister woodland glades, with rhododendrons and hydrangeas.

Columnar conifers, especially the slimmer ones, also excel as free-standing eyecatchers within the garden, as exclamation marks in the design. As an example, our own short blue-green chalkland juniper, *Juniperus communis* – at its best in the form 'Hibernica' – makes a terrific centrepiece for a prostrate mat of thymes and other alpine species. A dark Irish yew terminates a well-drained border or terrace beautifully, especially with the dome of a silver elaeagnus arching in front of it.

Italian cypress, *Cupressus sempervirens*, is hardy in all but the very coldest locations, growing well even at chilly Ickworth, Suffolk, in the company of sea buckthorn (*Hippophae*), a hardy substitute for olive. C. Stricta Group make chunky rockets, C. 'Totem Pole' is also dense, but as narrow as a cypress can be; I particularly like it running up the side of a sunny wall. Arizona cypress, C. *arizonica* 'Pyramidalis', gives you a column in silvery-blue.

I think the prince among mountain wilderness conifers is Serbian spruce, *Picea omorika*. With its tight habit and distinctively curved branches, it is one of the most striking of all trees. If I owned a stone Lakeland cottage, I would plant it as a sentinel.

And for contrasting with the willows of the waterside there are two deciduous conifers. The more obliging is Chinese dawn redwood, *Metasequoia glyptostroboides*, but if you have acid soil, then *Taxodium distichum* is your tree. This is the primeval swamp cypress of the southern United States. I had a happy afternoon in a Tennessee backwater among its knobbly root growths, which project like snorkels from the mud and water: the perfect antidote to my morning's visit to Graceland.

HEDGES AND CLIPPED SHAPES

Out in the countryside, wildflowers often play against a chequerboard of hedgerows, straight-edged woods, and lines of Lombardy poplar. And in the garden, you can strike equally dreamy contrasts with yew columns in meadow grass, box spirals in a woodland glade, and a pleached hornbeam walk through a gravel garden. On the other hand, you don't want to bequeath yourself hours of snipping, especially up a ladder.

Ideally, I like the superstructure of a garden to be as natural as possible, with the external boundaries made up of informal curtains of plants. This gives less of a sense of living in a compound. I do have one hedge and fence facing the road, but on the garden side, I am busy screening it away with maturing hollies.

In very small urban gardens, where there isn't enough elbow room for a border, conspicuous formal boundary lines are inevitable. So you want the most beautiful fence or hedge you can come up with. For a fence, I would be tempted by a combination of galvanized steel posts and woven hurdle panels, as employed by London designer Stephen Woodhams: very smart. While for hedges, my guru is Belgian designer Jacques Wirtz.

His house, at Schoten, near Antwerp, is hidden by the slimmest, most elegant hedge I have ever seen, a tall palisade of hornbeam, pruned back almost to the trunks and with edges kept razor sharp. He installed stout-stemmed plants several feet apart, and infilled with much thinner ones at 4–6 inch/10–15cm spacing, so the effect is like living railings, taking up very little space. Since hornbeam hangs on to its dead leaves through the winter, privacy is also well maintained.

Beech is the other top-notch deciduous formal material, and for a more rustic hedge (though a pretty threadbare one in winter) I would go for hawthorn, either neatly on its own or mixed, hedgerow-style, with blackthorn, holly, hazel and wild roses. *Berberis wilsoniae* is an exotic alternative. A short, dense, prickly Chinese bush, it exhibits a medley of leaf colours and coral fruits in autumn (set loose among the rocky cliff face, it is one of the seasonal highlights of Wakehurst Place, Kew's country outpost in Sussex).

For preference, though, I like my hedges and formal touches well inside the garden, creating ordered space within a wilder scene. The recipe can be seen in Jim Reynolds's garden near Trim, north of Dublin. His garden creates its own

↑ The rawness of the midwinter garden has its own beauty: almost all the emphasis is now on shape and line. In Tom Stuart-Smith's garden, warm-tinted beech hedges and seedheads (*top*) and box hedges like plumped-up cushions (*bottom*) make the scene very welcoming.

self-contained, rather magical world (in fact, I never found his house) – helped by the conversion of an outbuilding into a Rapunzel tower, complete with pointed roof and high lattice window.

Beneath the tower, box hedges make a formal spine down the centre of the garden, fringing straight paths and framing paved areas, but behind them are deep borders, frothing with meadowlike planting and receding into mysterious shrubbery and copse. And because you enter into the sunny, box-edged formality by way of meandering, shady pathways, there is a particularly strong sense of arrival, and of this being the very heart of the garden.

You can get a more relaxed and homely mood from your box hedges by giving them a rounded outline. Jacques Wirtz goes a stage further. Inside his Schoten garden, his box hedges billow and bulge like clouds scudding along the lawns and under the rows of apple trees. Old age, coupled with a period of neglect (before M. Wirtz's time), helped shape these quirky organic structures, which create mesmerizing patterns of shadow in sunlight and frost. But there is no reason why you couldn't achieve the effect quickly by planting bushes of different sizes and setting them askew. They give his garden a happy sense of what I call plump contentment.

The same mood is conveyed by the rippling yew hedges and jellymould yew lumps quivering on the terraces at Powis Castle, Welshpool. And I like the way some designers are now cutting the tops of yew hedges to make wavelike silhouettes, which echo the contours of distant hills. As a tall interior hedge, yew is in a class of its own, with a density and darkness that sets off flowers to perfection. Cypress is cheaper and faster, but a headache ever after.

Dwarf box, *Buxus sempervirens* 'Suffruticosa', is the most obliging low hedge and border edger, quite happy to support, and be smothered by, perennials for months on end without discolouring. Until recently, its only drawback was its scent, which many compare unfavourably to cat's pee. But now we have a virulent strain of fungal disease (*Cylindrocladium*) on the prowl, which causes plants to defoliate and, ultimately, die; pruning shears can spread it like wildfire. It has not visited me yet, so it's fingers crossed. As I write, there is no cure. Ordinary common box, used for taller hedges and topiaries, is less susceptible but not immune.

Gardens that have been hit by the fungus are now substituting box with evergreens like *Lonicera nitida* and *Ilex crenata*. On well-drained ground, you might also use lettuce-green *Hebe rakaiensis*: there is a run of it alongside a border of phormiums, grasses and white birches at Imperial College, just off Queen's Gate, South Kensington, which always catches my eye as I take a short cut to the parcels office.

Most hedging plants are put in at 18–24 inch/45–60cm spacing (half that for dwarf box) for quick effect, but double the spacing if you can; it gives each plant more root run, and is a lot cheaper. Clipping is best carried out in summer, but time it so it doesn't interfere with nesting birds. For this reason, we often end up doing our hedges in autumn or during a mild winter spell: the tall cypress hedge is like an avian apartment block.

STILT HEDGES AND AVENUES

A formal framework doesn't have to be monochrome, as the Herefordshire garden of Sir Roy Strong, ex-director of the Victoria & Albert Museum, and his wife, the stage designer Julia Trevelyan Oman, shows you. From the V & A temple (featuring the faces of Victoria, Albert and Sir Roy in the middle) to the Conservatory of Shame (built with the proceeds of a TV advert featuring Sir Roy), there is playful, Portmeirion-like theatre in these compartmented acres – the design, as a few visitors have observed, very much an echo of the V & A in its rooms and corridors, with objects on display.

Even in midwinter the garden is aglow. Admittedly much of the colour comes from the fact that any building or statue that can be gilded, or painted in blue, ochre or yellow, has been, including the house. But the structural plants don't sit around brooding, either.

I was so taken by the silhouettes of black-green Irish yew pillars against brilliant orange beech hedge that I immediately reproduced the combination back home. Glossy grass-green mounds of cherry laurel were also a cheery sight against the beech and yew. But most arresting of all was the haze of scarlet twigs on top of the pleached hedges of lime, *Tilia platyphyllos* 'Rubra'.

Pleached hedges – lines of straight-trunked young trees, planted at a 6ft/2m or wider spacing, with branches trained to form hedges on stilts – are a very classy addition to a garden. Here they flank a path, but plants can also be woven into a square or circular centrepiece, perhaps over gravel, as a bower, or as a frame for a small front garden. But they are fairly demanding, requiring an initial supporting structure of posts and wires, as well as annual pruning and tying-in.

A miniature avenue or phalanx of trees can play a similar formal role. The mophead robinia, *Robinia pseudoacacia* 'Umbraculifera', can easily be kept to parasol height or less. And at Overbecks, in Sharpitor, Devon, there is an entrance avenue of hardy, slow-growing Chusan palm, *Trachycarpus fortunei*, setting a ritzy Riviera tone.

FORMAL PUNCTUATION

Like hedges, free-standing formal shapes can also help to organize and frame a view. Box cones and balls are traditionally used to mark the ends of borders or to punctuate a gravel courtyard. And you often see a line of vertical, black-green Irish yews dividing sections of lawn, or separating lawn from border – particularly striking above a drop in level.

At Wallington, Northumberland, fastigiate golden yews, *Taxus baccata* 'Standishii', march along the terrace wall, nicely partnered with white martagon lilies. And on a raised grass bank at Haseley Court, south of Oxford, Irish yews alternate with globes of Portugal laurel to frame a topiary chess set below, made of box and English yew.

Gardens do not come much more stylish than Haseley Court. The late Nancy Lancaster, doyenne of the Colefax & Fowler interior design company, was the guiding spirit here. A Virginian by birth, she would fly the Confederate

→ Lopsided spirals of yew, on the corners of the lawn, add quirky touches to the formal framework of Haseley Court, seen through the Confederate grey gazebo.

flag from the house, and had the garden doors and seats painted Confederate grey.

She had *l'art de vivre* well sorted. It was revealed in a TV documentary that she started her day with her butler bringing her breakfast in bed, and playing her a recording of the dawn chorus. The three essentials for a welcoming room, she said, are an open fire, candles, and a vase of garden flowers – the other essential, luxurious furnishings, was taken for granted.

She used free-standing topiaries throughout Haseley Court, to punctuate the design and maintain a sense of order in winter. One herbaceous border has yew buttresses projecting at intervals from the wall, while the path running alongside it is broken half-way down its length by flanking pairs of yew cubes. The small lawn in the walled garden has box spirals on two of its corners. And entrances are invariably flanked by box or rich green English yew shapes; or, beside one gateway, a pair of fastigiate 'Skyrocket' junipers (a bit anorexic for me).

Holly clips well into large cylinders (as do beech and hornbeam). I have one beside the drive at home. And along a shady path, I grow a pair of sweet bays in half-barrels, clipped as umbrellas to flank a bench. Portugal laurel is used like this at Hidcote. There are many plants you can formalize.

On the whole, my own taste is for geometric rather than whimsical shapes, though I was rather taken with the flock of topiary chickens and eggs I once saw in Holland, and the yew bison grazing in a Nashville meadow.

BACKDROP EVERGREENS

Free-form evergreen and deciduous shrubs, in naturalistic groupings, serve as the other principal boundary building blocks. It is the evergreens I like to place first, to ensure there is an appealing winter framework and the defences are where I want them.

I think the best boundary evergreens are the shadowy ones, those with dark green foliage. Given enough elbow room, my recommendation for quick privacy is Portugal laurel, *Prunus lusitanica*. It could pass as a native, will grow in sun or shade on pretty much any soil, including chalk and clay, and with a bit of moisture will race away almost as fast as Leyland cypress. And yet it stops at 25ft/7.5m instead of 125ft/37m. It sports vanilla-scented white streamers in summer, has fetching red leaf stems, and can be clipped to almost any shape. A paragon, in other words. There is also a handsome small-leaved version, 'Myrtifolia'.

The shorter, slow-growing, evergreen viburnum *V. tinus* blends well with it, and gives white flowers in winter (though I'm not too keen on the smell). I have them in tandem behind a pale eucalyptus trunk. And both make good textural contrast in front of a feathery screening conifer or blue-green pine.

Holly is a perfect backdrop evergreen, though it takes its time. The prickly sorts are handy for discouraging intruders and vandals, but devils to weed around; *Ilex × altaclerensis* 'Atkinsonii' is a broad-leaved one (male). Otherwise, I use smooth-edged *I. aquifolium* 'J. C. van Tol' and the upright 'Pyramidalis' (both female, and therefore, when pollinated by a male, carrying red berries).

You get a spotty winter effect if you mix evergreen and deciduous shrubs too erratically. I try to plant alternating passages: a group of low deciduous shrubs, backed by a drift of mid-height evergreens, backed by a stand of deciduous trees, that sort of thing. You can also tell by the above little list that I prefer the garden backdrop not to be too fancy. Instead, I like to suggest a transition into the countryside – even though, in my case, that is a couple of miles away. But in smaller gardens, you may resent sacrificing ground to these more pedestrian shrubs, in which case, read on . . .

BACKBONE EVERGREENS

It is in the nature of some habitats, like meadows and prairies, to be fairly free of shrubs, so you don't necessarily want to stuff evergreens into every border. Instead, the winter look in some parts of the garden might simply consist of open drifts of parchment-tinted grasses, perennial seedheads and bare soil, either formally framed by box edging and yew shapes, or with a belt of shrubs some way behind, to give the sense of meadow meeting wood. A lone tree, juniper, or deciduous shrub might add a further silhouette.

Likewise, a pondside may simply feature bullrushes, interrupted by a thicket of pollarded willow, or a solitary twisted hazel, *Corylus avellana* 'Contorta', dripping catkins. (Though I do like the formal use of fat, well-spaced clumps of sword-leaved *Phormium tenax*, which bring winter order to the moist herbaceous border at Bodnant, North Wales.)

Here and there, you can also achieve a welcome variation in your winter scene by having evergreens as a carpet at ground level, instead of as mid-height to tall shrubs – a sweep of heather, low rhododendrons, evergreen ferns or pachysandra, for example, perhaps spiked by a birch or a magnolia.

Where you do plant sizeable evergreens to put backbone into a border, it often pays to go the whole hog and to plant several close together – either of the same species, or a contrast: the exotic shapes of bamboo, phormium, and fatsia, for instance, or the emerald of Mexican orange blossom beside the yellow-splashed holly *Ilex × altaclerensis* 'Lawsoniana'. That way you get a decent winter picture. I often add a bare-branched winter-bloomer to the mix, such as pink *Viburnum × bodnantense* between black-stemmed bamboo and hummocky sarcococca.

EVERGREENS IN SHADE

Shady borders and north walls are bound to end up with a good complement of evergreens: evergreen leaves being an adaptation to low light levels, the world's forests abound in them.

In the sunnier of my two long woodland glade borders here at home, *Osmanthus × burkwoodii* is the lynchpin. The vanilla scent that its white stars pump out in April coincides with that moment when the wild cherries are in blossom and the blackbirds are gurgling; give me warm sun, and I am

→ *Skimmia × confusa* 'Kew Green' is a good punctuation shrub for the front of shady borders. The flowerheads contribute in winter and spring, but it is male, so there are no berries.

in orbit. Slowly, it forms a dense, upright, 10ft/3m cloud of small, dark leaves.

It stands at the back of the border beside a pink-berried Asian rowan tree, and behind evergreen *Viburnum* × *burkwoodii*. The most flower-packed specimen of this viburnum I have ever seen, smothered in clove-scented balls, was out in the open under the blazing Australian sun, but, like osmanthus, it adapts well to part shade and doesn't jar in a woodland setting. I keep its dome of glossy, mid-green leaves to around 6ft/2m.

This trio then connects, by means of the bare stems of a red tree peony, *P. delavayi*, and the antlers of a stag's-horn sumach, to a foreground partnership of red-flowered *Skimmia japonica* 'Rubella' and scarlet-stemmed dogwood (the soil drops in level, and gets quite heavy). I plug the winter gap around the deciduous peony and sumach with a wooden obelisk, which I move around the border like a chess piece, putting it wherever I think it looks best that season. In this, I take my cue from Stowe Landscape Garden in Buckinghamshire, except there the family used to move whole temples around on whim.

My formula in this border has been to use shrubs to build a more or less continuous background ridge, which descends in height to form three promontories, one in the middle of the border and one at each end. The promontories are set on a slight diagonal, which I prefer to rigid right angles, and the two wide bays between them are filled with perennials and bulbs.

But here and there you are also likely to want solo evergreens, to serve as punctuation points in the design. Dense, compact shapes are the smartest. *Mahonia japonica* plays the role at Knightshayes, Devon, under the north-facing wall of the house. Naturally multi-stemmed, it is as sculptural as a small tree, and stands at each end of a long bed, rising from a mat of alchemilla and yellow epimedium (a handsome leaf marriage in spring).

Palm-like *Fatsia japonica* is also an impressive solo act, especially in autumn when it is sporting cream drumsticks, but it needs shelter and a mild climate to give of its best. Pairs of them stand in front of the Guards barracks by Buckingham Palace, permanently on parade.

To act as short 'full-stop' plants at the front of shady borders, I rely on skimmias, variegated box ('Elegantissima'), native butcher's broom (*Ruscus*), *Viburnum davidii* and sarcococca. This last is pressed into service on several of my path junctions. *S. confusa* is fresh green, 2–3ft/60–100cm in height, *S. hookeriana* var. *humilis* is shorter and darker. Both exude a heavy honey scent in February.

EVERGREENS FOR SHADY BORDERS AND WOODLAND GLADES

Asplenium	Fatsia	Osmanthus	Viburnum
Aucuba	Gaultheria	Pieris	burkwoodii
Blechnum	Ilex	Rhododendron	Viburnum davidii
Buxus	Kalmia	Ruscus	Viburnum
Camellia	Libertia	Sarcococca	rhytidophyllum
Daphniphyllum	Ligustrum	Skimmia	
Eucryphia	Mahonia	Trochodendron	

EVERGREENS FOR SHADY WALLS

Euonymus fortunei	Hedera	Pileostegia	Pyracantha

The other areas of the garden asking to be cloaked in evergreen shrubs are the sunny, well-drained spots. The warm, scrubby hillsides of the world (the Mediterranean, California, Chile, China, New Zealand . . .) are bristling with evergreen contenders. And not all of them are green. There are silvers, greys and blues to play with here; the odd natural gold, too, like *Hebe ochracea*, and winter crimson, like *Bergenia purpurascens*. There is also quite a range of leaf shapes, textures and habits.

So you can weave an interesting winter tapestry, and you don't get that heavy look which often comes when woodland evergreens are planted *en masse*. In the walled gravel garden at Denmans, Sussex, originally set out by the late Joyce Robinson (the gravel scrunching as she belted about in her electric wheelchair), there is an inspired backbone partnership featuring dark ceanothus, blue-green *Euphorbia characias* subsp. *wulfenii*, glossy Mexican orange blossom, and a clipped mound of cream-variegated box. That not only gives plenty of leaf contrast in winter, but a stunning simultaneous blue, lime-yellow, and white flower display in May.

On a more modest scale, I am rather pleased with my own teaming of *Cistus* × *cyprius* (a 6ft/2m dome of broad, metallic grey-green leaves) with the feathery, upright Mount Etna broom, and the emerald discs of griselinia with black-green Irish yew.

Because there are so many good, and varied, mid-height and front row evergreens, I think of the shrubby backbone for well-drained, sunny sites less in terms of ridge and promontory, and more as numerous tentacles which descend in height from front to back, and wriggle right through the border. For instance, one tentacle might start with dark *Cistus* × *cyprius*, then drop into silvery senecio (*Brachyglottis* 'Sunshine' we are supposed to call it now), blue *Euphorbia characias* 'Lambrook Yellow', and prickly mounds of Spanish gorse (*Genista hispanica*), before finishing as a little squiggle of shrubby and prostrate thymes. In between the tentacles go the bulbs and perennials.

For a neat foreground evergreen to use on its own, either in cloudlike formation through the middle of a border, or as punctuation points at the ends, I would turn to hebes. *H. rakaiensis* is lime-green, *H. topiaria* is grey-green, and *H. cupressoides* is blue-grey and, unexpectedly, scented of cedar. They look good next to phormiums.

Yuccas and bergenias were a favourite end-of-border pairing of the sainted Gertrude Jekyll, and they make equally rewarding theme plants for an informal gravel garden, the bergenia running along the meandering path edges, as in Beth Chatto's garden, and the yuccas midway back in widely spaced groups.

Yuccas were the eyecatchers in the wild, shrubby hills I explored above Los Angeles, their white flower plumes like smoke signals against the dry banks of sticky orange *Mimulus aurantiacus* and other aromatic shrubs. Watching the hummingbirds spiralling in courtship display, you would never guess there was a world of drugs, murder and mugging only fifteen minutes away.

BROADLEAVED EVERGREENS FOR GRAVEL GARDEN AND SUNNY TERRACE

Arbutus	Cotoneaster	Helleborus	Olearia
Berberis	Drimys	argutifolius	Osmanthus
Bergenia	Elaeagnus	Laurus	Phillyrea
Brachyglottis	Escallonia	Libertia	Rosmarinus
Buxus	Euphorbia	Ligustrum	Ruta
Choisya	Griselinia	Lonicera nitida	Yucca
Cistus	Hebe	Myrtus	

EVERGREENS FOR SUNNY WALLS

Azara	Garrya	Pittosporum	Trachelospermum
Ceanothus	Itea	Pyracantha	
Clematis armandii	Magnolia grandiflora	Stauntonia	

← The transformation of *Euphorbia characias* subsp. *wulfenii* from tight, purple-flushed croziers into cylinders of green frogspawn keeps you entertained for many weeks.

6 — THE PROCESS OF PLANTING

I do very little planning on paper. It is much easier to make lists of plants, and combinations of plants, that you want to grow and then assemble them on the ground, piece by piece like a jigsaw.

And while professional designers are forced to install everything in one fell swoop, the home gardener can savour the job, with plenty of whisky-fumed evenings of reading and rumination, and weekend nursery visits along the way. The beauty of being offered plants for sale in containers is that you can readily stagger the planting process (and the expense) over many weeks and months, and take it step by step, one idea and one season at a time.

LYNCHPIN SHAPES

Since there is no set way of tackling things, it is every man for himself. As I have already outlined, I suggest kicking off with the big picture: the garden's major eyecatchers and structural elements.

Once down to the scale of an individual border, I would see if these need supplementing with further winter silhouettes and evergreens, to forge a scene within a scene – perhaps a bonfire of scarlet-stemmed dogwood, *Cornus alba* 'Sibirica', to animate a dull corner by the lawn, or a drift of finely-cut *Helleborus foetidus* Wester Flisk Group to fill the empty foreground of a wide flower-bed (actually, the dogwood and hellebore look rather good together, especially with snowdrops thrown in).

But as the growing season advances, the impact of many of these winter

← Previous page: The purplish foliage of *Fuchsia* 'Thalia' (three bushy plants grown in one large pot) reinforces the impact of *Acer griseum* in my summer border. The wooden pyramid is portable, and moves along the border wherever a temporary eyecatcher is required.

← Left: Scarlet dogwood, *Cornus alba* 'Sibirica', is inconspicuous during the summer, but when the leaves drop, it is one of the garden's most potent beacons. The pyramid joins it for a few weeks.

features is reduced, even lost. So a few extra summer eyecatchers, in the form of herbaceous plants with a striking outline, and shrubs with bold or colourful deciduous foliage, probably need to be inserted.

What you want is for each view to have a major focal point, discernible even in the jungle of August, and to have markers along the way which punctuate the planting into readable chunks.

Contrast is the key to a good marker. At Lady Farm, it is the slim stems and feathery flowerheads of the giant oat grass, *Stipa gigantea*, and, further down the slope, of the early-blooming pampas grass, *Cortaderia richardii*, that lead the eye along the stream garden. They last for months. Their impact comes from the fact that each clump is isolated between rocks and lawn, with a fountain-like habit that has nothing in common with the dense, rounded shrub masses beyond. (Miscanthus grasses make good fountains, too.)

Poor old pampas. It still brings out the same embarrassed giggles as the flight of china ducks up the sitting-room wall. Time it was rehabilitated, I think, and embraced into the current grasses craze, not least for the fact that the South American sorts (*C. richardii* is a New Zealander) are at their brightest through the dimmest part of the year, when hardly anything else is bothering to turn out. Tall *C. selloana* 'Sunningdale Silver' and 5ft/1.5m *C. s.* 'Pumila' are two of the best. Their vertical shapes are as dramatic and exclamatory in the landscape as fastigiate conifers, white bramble stems (*Rubus*), and pale birch trunks.

In a garden on Chesapeake Bay, Maryland, James van Sweden relies on another grass, the mid-height *Calamagrostis × acutiflora* 'Karl Foerster', as his vertical contrast. He threads a thin, transparent line of it between broad flat planes of swimming-pool and decking, mown lawn and the Bay. Nothing else intrudes, apart from a painted boathouse. It has become one of the most admired minimalist scenes in gardening.

Asceticism is not taken to extremes, though. Around the sides of the house, I found the borders stuffed, which was a relief. You can't live without comforts and curios. I once watched a TV programme on people who lived in minimalist houses. Serenity on the surface, but cupboards and cellars exploding with clobber.

→ A bold horizontal line is as arresting as a vertical, as demonstrated by this glade of *Cornus controversa* 'Variegata' at The Garden House.

Emphatically horizontal plants are equally eyecatching, none more so than the wedding-cake dogwoods. Keith Wiley has planted a trio of them – white-splashed *Cornus controversa* 'Variegata' – in a dell of low shrubs and ground-cover at The Garden House. The scale of the vista demanded a major reference point, and horizontals always stand out well like this, isolated in the centre of a garden or border, with taller plants arranged some way back. I have the more compact wedding cake, *C. alternifolia* 'Argentea', presiding over one of my glades.

Set next to bold verticals, horizontals make a powerful impression, in the manner of that simple slab of slate, placed as a seat among the columns of tree trunks at Holker Hall, Cumbria. Connect several horizontals together – a tiered mahonia and a 'Wilhelm Pfitzer' juniper overhanging a sheet of water, covered with flat rafts of waterlilies, for example – and you have a striking structural line through your planting.

The other point to make about horizontals is that they are transformed when seen from above. This hit home while I was standing on the roof of a bank in Munich (don't ask), looking down on to a garden created in a light well, a sort of outdoor atrium, in which another dogwood, *C. kousa*, was in full bloom. The full wonder of those tiers of upward-facing creamy flowers, usually seen only by birds and low-flying aircraft, was mine for the first time.

A few months later I was peering out of someone's bathroom window on to

a pool of purple lacecap flowers, being sported by the big August hydrangeas *H. aspera* Villosa Group and *H. a.* subsp. *sargentiana*. Again, I had never realized they were so handsome. (Another group of shrubs with flat flowerheads, though again not with an overall horizontal branch structure, are the elders, *Sambucus*.)

ATTRACTIVE PLANTS WITH A BOLD HORIZONTAL OUTLINE

- *Cornus alternifolia* 'Argentea'
- *Cornus controversa* 'Variegata'
- *Cotoneaster horizontalis*
- *Hamamelis* × *intermedia* 'Pallida'
- *Juniperus* × *pfitzeriana* 'William Pfitzer'
- *Juniperus sabina* 'Tamariscifolia'
- *Mahonia japonica*
- *Mahonia* × *media* cultivars
- *Prunus laurocerasus* 'Zabeliana'
- *Viburnum plicatum* 'Mariesii'

PERENNIALS

Achillea filipendulina 'Gold Plate' *Sedum* 'Herbstfreude'

Huge leaves make very potent markers. They are mostly associated with moisture, cool shade, and sunny waterside, but glossy green acanthus, bergenia, grey cardoon (*Cynara*), and *Crambe cordifolia*, with its giant gypsophila-like white flower cloud, enjoy well-drained ground. Crambe

leaves become less potent as summer advances (Gertrude Jekyll used to train an August clematis through its spent flowerhead), as do those of the ornamental rhubarb, *Rheum palmatum* 'Atrosanguineum'. Its crimson foliage is a jaw-dropping sight among the bulbs and emerging perennials of spring, accompanied by those monster red flowerheads (extremely phallic early on).

Tropical leaves, such as those of cannas, alocasias, ricinus and bananas, can rescue a border in late summer in spectacular style. I remember the translucent shields of the red-backed, red-veined dwarf banana *Ensete ventri-cosum*, commanding a view of exotically planted pools below the deck of Dennis Schrader and Bill Smith's clapboard house on Long Island, New York. It was autumn, and as the sun began sinking, flocks of migrating orange monarch butterflies started clustering in the branches of a tree behind – communal warmth to help them through the chilly night. The next day, Long Island got the tail end of a hurricane, and the banana was shredded; I hope not the butterflies.

ATTRACTIVE PLANTS WITH LARGE LEAVES

SHRUBS

Aralia elata	Hydrangea aspera	Paulownia tomentosa
Catalpa bignonioides	'Macrophylla'	(pollarded)
(pollarded)	Hydrangea aspera subsp.	
	sargentiana	

CLIMBERS

Clematis armandii	Vitis coignetiae

EXOTICS

Agave	Datura	Ricinus
Alocasia	Dicksonia antarctica	Solanum quitoense
Canna	Melianthus major	

PERENNIALS

Acanthus mollis	Darmera peltata	Macleaya microcarpa
Acanthus spinosus	Gunnera manicata	'Kelway's Coral Plume'
Bergenia	Hosta (especially H.	Osmunda regalis
Cardiocrinum giganteum	sieboldiana varieties)	Podophyllum peltatum
Crambe cordifolia	Ligularia dentata	Rheum palmatum
Crocosmia 'Lucifer' and	Lysichiton	'Atrosanguineum'
other cultivars	Macleaya cordata	Rodgersia
Cynara cardunculus		Veratrum

Glaucous-blue *Melianthus major* gives dashing half-hardy back-up for well-drained ground, as does silver-speared *Astelia chathamica* (good among rugs of

← The soft, silver-haired leaves of the unusual *Bergenia ciliata* develop after its pink flowers have faded in spring, and can grow to the size of dinner plates in a sheltered shady spot.

grey *Anthemis punctata* subsp. *cupaniana* at the Dorothy Clive Garden, Staffordshire). And to give foreground definition in her gravel garden, Beth Chatto inserts pots of green and variegated dagger-leaved *Agave americana* among her rugs of thymes, sages and silver artemisias.

Although agaves don't grow to the sizes you see them in Mexico, where they are often planted around estancias as a bandit-proof stockade, they can get pretty hefty. It takes two of us to lug mine indoors for the winter – but with less pain than previously, thanks to a reader who suggested I stick wine corks on to the spines.

LYNCHPIN LEAF COLOUR

A mass of contrasting leaf colour is even more attention-grabbing than shape. A burst of silver among greens, and of green among silvers, are the principal contrasts that spring from nature's colour palette, and they will feature strongly in later chapters. But there is also the option of more theatrical contrasts, centred on all those gold, variegated and purple freaks of nature painstakingly propagated by gardeners over the years. They are fun, but since they can easily Disneyfy the mood it is wise to use them sparingly, in designated spots.

Golds I usually put in the shadiest place I can get away with, to give the impression of filtered sunshine. They won't colour up in darkness, but part-shade persuades many of them, including choisya and hostas, to take on a chartreuse glow, which I prefer to the brash tints you get in bright light.

There is a corner at Haseley Court, Oxfordshire, where golden hop twines through a lattice wooden pyramid, in the Confederate grey livery, with golden feverfew (*Tanacetum*) seeding through silver stachys below and the big lime-green shields of *Hosta plantaginea* as a 2ft/60cm counterweight. It is a perfect piece of planting design.

Golden philadelphus is my favourite golden shrub, a clean and brilliant ripe lemon to set beside orange berberis among the emerging greens. At Haseley, it stands either side of the oak bench at the end of the laburnum tunnel, so you are encouraged to linger and drink in its fruity fragrance. Scents and seats go together like the proverbial horse and carriage.

ATTRACTIVE PLANTS WITH BOLD GOLDEN LEAVES

SHRUBS

- *Acer shirasawanum* 'Aureum'
- *Berberis thunbergii* 'Aurea'
- *Calluna* cultivars
- *Cornus alba* 'Aurea'
- *Hebe ochracea* 'James Stirling'
- *Ligustrum* 'Vicaryi'
- *Lonicera nitida* 'Baggesen's Gold'
- *Philadelphus coronarius* 'Aureus'
- *Rubus cockburnianus* 'Goldenvale'
- *Sambucus racemosa* 'Plumosa Aurea'
- *Spiraea japonica* 'Goldflame'
- *Taxus baccata* 'Semperaurea'
- *Taxus baccata* 'Standishii'

CLIMBERS

- *Hedera helix* 'Buttercup'
- *Humulus lupulus* 'Aureus'

PERENNIALS

Acanthus mollis 'Hollard's Gold'
Filipendula ulmaris 'Aurea'
Hosta 'Sum and Substance'

Hosta 'Zounds'
Lysimachia nummularia 'Aurea'
Tanacetum parthenium 'Aureum'

GRASSES

Carex elata 'Aurea'
Milium effusum 'Aureum'

Luzula sylvatica 'Aurea'
Luzula sylvatica 'Hohe Tatra'

I am even more cautious with variegated leaves. They have immediate appeal in the garden centre, but sprinkle them through your borders and it can be a bit like living with paparazzi: camera flash-bulbs going off all the time. Group them all together, and you get steadier illumination and a proper design flourish.

I like to weave plain green and golden leaves through them. Gold and white variegated foliage is a favourite mix of mine. Bowles' golden grass (*Milium*) filters through spotted pulmonarias in the shady bed by the front door, with golden philadelphus standing next to white-edged holly.

ATTRACTIVE PLANTS WITH BOLD VARIEGATED LEAVES

*yellow or cream variegation; all others have white markings

SHRUBS

- *Aralia elata* 'Aureovariegata'*
- *Aralia elata* 'Variegata'
- *Buxus sempervirens* 'Elegantissima'*
- *Cornus alba* 'Spaethii'*
- *Cornus alternifolia* 'Argentea'
- *Cornus controversa* 'Variegata'
- *Elaeagnus pungens* 'Maculata'*
- *Ilex aquifolium* 'Ferox Argentea'
- *Ilex aquifolium* 'Golden Queen'*
- *Ilex aquifolium* 'Silver King'
- *Ilex × altaclerensis* 'Golden King'*
- *Ilex × altaclerensis* 'Lawsoniana'*
- *Ligustrum lucidum* 'Excelsum Superbum'*
- *Pachysandra terminalis* 'Variegata'
- *Philadelphus coronarius* 'Variegatus'
- *Rhamnus alaternus* 'Argenteovariegata'
- *Salvia officinalis* 'Icterina'*
- *Salvia officinalis* 'Tricolor'
- *Sambucus nigra* 'Aureomarginata'*
- *Stachyurus* 'Magpie'
- *Viburnum tinus* 'Variegatum'*
- *Vinca major* 'Variegata'*
- *Vinca minor* 'Argenteovariegata'

CLIMBERS

- *Hedera canariensis* 'Gloire de Marengo'
- *Hedera colchica* 'Dentata Variegata'*
- *Hedera colchica* 'Sulphur Heart'*
- *Hedera helix* 'Glacier'
- *Hedera helix* 'Oro di Bogliasco' (syn. *H. h.* 'Goldheart')*
- *Jasminum officinale* 'Argenteovariegatum'
- *Lonicera japonica* 'Aureoreticulata'*
- *Trachelospermum jasminoides* 'Variegatum'

PERENNIALS

Arum italicum 'Marmoratum'
Astrantia major 'Sunningdale Variegated'
Brunnera macrophylla 'Dawson's White'
Brunnera macrophylla 'Hadspen Cream'
Hosta fortunei 'Albopicta'*
Hosta fortunei 'Aureomarginata'*
Hosta fortunei 'Francee'
Hosta fortunei 'Gold Standard'*
Hosta fortunei 'June'*
Hosta montana 'Aureomarginata'*
Hosta sieboldiana 'Frances Williams'*
Hosta ventricosa 'Aureomaculata'*

Iris foetidissima 'Variegata'
Iris pallida 'Aureovariegata'*
Iris pallida 'Variegata'
Iris pseudacorus 'Variegatus'*
Mentha × gracilis 'Variegata'
Phormium cookianum 'Cream Delight'*
Phormium cookianum 'Yellow Wave'*
Scrophularia aquatica 'Variegata'
Sisyrinchium striatum 'Aunt May'*
Symphytum × uplandicum 'Variegatum'*
Yucca flaccida 'Golden Sword'*
Yucca gloriosa 'Variegata'*

In another variegated patch, I use yellow flowers, notably the mid-height summer daisy *Inula hookeri*, which flops around the verticals of white-striped miscanthus grass and white-veined snakebark maple. Its own thin petals add to the linear harmony. This was serendipity.

As with golden leaves, variegated foliage is at its best in part shade, though the sages (*Salvia*), *Iris pallida*, and iris-like *Sisyrinchium striatum* 'Aunt May' are, like molinia and pampas grasses, emphatic sun-lovers.

Purple is a shadow colour, for suggesting background depth and throwing pale colours into relief. Too much of it is depressing.

Some leaves, like those of elders (*Sambucus*) and pittosporums, can verge on black, but the only really black hardy plant is the ground-hugging lily turf, *Ophiopogon planiscapus* 'Nigrescens'. With black berries as well as black grass-like leaves, it is a much more entertaining alternative to bugle (*Ajuga*) to spread as a carpet alongside a path, perhaps with black-stemmed bamboo and blue hostas sprouting through. It holds its colour even in quite deep shade.

I realized how you get it to luxuriate on a visit to the Bloedel Reserve, on Bainbridge Island, west of Seattle: plenty of moisture. The rainfall is so high there that the forested grounds are thick with lime-green moss, and at the

↑ *Phormium* 'Yellow Wave' is a dashing plant, and worth risking outside in all but the coldest gardens.

ATTRACTIVE PLANTS WITH BOLD PURPLE AND RED LEAVES

SHRUBS

- *Acer palmatum* 'Atropurpureum'
- *Acer palmatum* Dissectum Atropurpureum Group
- *Berberis* × *ottawensis* 'Superba'
- *Berberis thunbergii* 'Atropurpurea Nana'
- *Berberis thunbergii* f. *atropurpurea*
- *Berberis thunbergii* 'Red Chief'
- *Cercis canadensis* 'Forest Pansy'
- *Corylus maxima* 'Purpurea'
- *Cotinus coggygria* 'Royal Purple'
- *Pittosporum tenuifolium* 'Purpureum'
- *Pittosporum tenuifolium* 'Tom Thumb'
- *Prunus* × *cistena*
- *Prunus spinosa* 'Purpurea'
- *Rosa glauca*
- *Salvia officinalis* 'Purpurascens'
- *Sambucus nigra* 'Guincho Purple'

CLIMBERS

- *Hedera helix* 'Atropurpurea'
- *Vitis vinifera* 'Purpurea'

ANNUALS

Atriplex hortensis var. *rubra*

Ricinus

PERENNIALS

Actaea (Cimicifuga) simplex 'Brunette'

Ajuga reptans 'Atropurpurea'

Aster lateriflorus 'Prince'

Euphorbia dulcis 'Chameleon'

Foeniculum vulgare 'Purpureum'

Heuchera micrantha 'Bressingham Bronze'

Ligularia dentata 'Desdemona'

Lysimachia ciliata 'Firecracker'

Ophiopogon planiscapus 'Nigrescens'

Phormium 'Sundowner'

Phormium tenax Purpureum Group

Sedum telephium 'Atropurpureum'

Sedum telephium 'Vera Jameson'

Sempervivum cultivars

Viola riviniana 'Purpurea'

GRASS

Imperata cylindrica 'Rubra'

TENDER EXOTICS

Aeonium arboreum 'Zwartkop'

Canna cultivars

Cordyline australis 'Atropurpurea'

entrance to the Japanese garden I met the best runs of lily turf I had ever seen, sandwiched between the moss and a run of dark grey cobbles. My friend Terri Clark and I turned out to be just about the only people exploring those eighty

enchanted acres, the silence broken only by some strange metallic parps, which we traced to a mating pair of trumpeter swans.

On the whole, we think of purple foliage as sun-loving, though many plants do remain potent in part shade. At Chirk Castle, a purple Japanese maple draws the eye into a moist woodland glade of hydrangeas, blue hostas and blue *Iris sibirica*. And here at home, I have a stand of purple-leaved *Actaea* (*Cimicifuga*) *simplex* 'Brunette' (scrumptious bubblegum scent from its long white bottlebrushes) as a full stop to a drift of autumn asters, which gets no more than an hour a day of full sunshine.

But certainly, purple leaves come to life when they are backlit by the sun. Purple-leaved vine, for example, is a gloomy old thing on a wall, but put it on a trellis or pergola where you can see through it, and it turns ruby. Purple smoke bush (*Cotinus*) goes through the same change when free-standing in a border.

↑ *Ophiopogon planiscapus* 'Nigrescens' combines with *Hosta* 'Halcyon' in a part-shaded corner of my garden.

An elegant shrub, it is well sited at Lytes Cary, Somerset, as the centrepiece to a bed of catmint and grey-purple sage, spiked by self-seeding red orach (*Atriplex*).

COMPOSING THE SEASONAL PICTURES

Once all the building blocks are in place, it is a matter of filling the empty spaces in between. This is where the 'seasonal pictures' I mentioned earlier come in, and they are the subject of the rest of this book. There are endless

combinations of plants you can come up with, but you can break down the design and thought process into logical steps.

For each space, I recommend first deciding on a principal and, if possible, secondary flowering period (which means leaving space for bulbs, an odd shrub, or a few clumps of perennials with a different season). You must also decide which colours and shapes will be dominant.

After that, you take it plant by plant. You start with something charismatic, which may be one of your existing evergreens or eyecatchers, or it may be a fantastic ephemeral like a rambler rose or a red hot poker, which you now insert. Next, you select a companion that plays well against it in flower or leaf.

Then, you choose another plant that looks good next to that; and so on, like assembling a jigsaw.

As you proceed, you make sure there is enough contrast of shape to tide you over the quiet periods, and that there are enough harmonious echoes of colour and form to knit everything together.

This approach works even if you are orchestrating a more mingled, meadowlike picture. You start with one of the key repeating or rhythmic plants, perhaps a grass; then you weave through a complementary plant; then another; then another . . .

There is no hurry. Why not shop for one plant at a time? And since a great many plants can be bought either in flower, or from nurseries with display gardens, there needn't be a ruinous amount of trial and error involved in getting the picture right.

If you are not starting with bare ground, but rather with a muddle of inherited shrubs and perennials, I would transfer everything desirable and movable into a holding bed, and reintroduce them into the border one at a time. It sounds a palaver, but I find it is the only hope of seeing the wood for the trees.

Inevitably there will be impulse buys which don't correspond to any of your original ideas. The procedure with them is the same as for plants growing in the wrong place. Pick a flower and a leaf, wander around testing it against other colours and shapes until you hit on the perfect spot, and see if you can shoehorn it in.

If there are to be deciduous shrubs in the planting, it is sensible to place them before placing perennials. Bulbs, annuals and bedding go in last.

A WORD ABOUT DECIDUOUS SHRUBS

Deciduous shrubs may give just one or two bursts of amazing flower and leaf colour during the year, or they may tick over pleasantly, spring to autumn, without ever quite stopping the traffic (the bushy elm, *Ulmus* × *elegantissima*

← | Previous page: Swathes of aquilegias and geraniums create an early summer spectacle between the building blocks of evergreen shrubs, church tower and birch trunks at The Garden House.

'Jacqueline Hillier', for example). Either way, they can take up a fair bit of space and become quite prominent objects in the design.

The main distinction I make is between shrubs that contribute to the July to September perennial season and those that don't. Most of the larger winter-, spring- and early summer-flowering shrubs are undistinguished, amorphous lumps later. The best place for them by mid-July is fading into the background.

A certain amount of mileage can be had by contrasting their shapes and leaves with neighbouring evergreens (philadelphus showering over *Cotoneaster horizontalis*, say), but I wouldn't make a big stand of them anywhere, and definitely they shouldn't be allowed to sit brooding in areas which are trying to look chirpy through the summer. Instead, I would keep them to the fringes, massing winter and spring bulbs and shade-tolerant perennials under their canopy. Not planting bulbs underneath deciduous shrubs is a criminal waste of opportunity.

Some bulky shrubs do pull their weight after they have flowered. These are the species with handsome foliage, like the cut-leaved tree peonies, *Paeonia delavayi* var. *ludlowii* and its kin, and shimmery silver-leaved *Elaeagnus commutata*; and the species that give a summer display of fruits, like the shrub roses *Rosa* 'Geranium' and *R.* 'Highdownensis', which shower vermilion hips over the terraces at Powis Castle. Planted as an early-season appetizer among meadow perennials, they won't detract when the perennials are themselves in bloom a couple of months later.

'It is no good having everything happening over three weeks during the summer. Winter should be fun.' I can hear the late Esther Merton, who gardened at Burghfield, near Reading, saying this, as, escaping from the clutches of her live-in nurse ('Nurse Knockout'), accompanied by her two pugs Hugo and Algy, she conducts wide-eyed visitors past her husband's beloved rhododendron hybrids ('Ralph's tarts') in her wheelchair and around the lake to the sheets of snowdrops and hellebores spread under the trees.

Winter is a long season in Britain, but, thanks to our relatively mild temperatures, a lot of flower action can be programmed to keep the spirits up, at least after New Year. November and December are trickier.

EXTERIOR DÉCOR FOR EARLY WINTER

With the dropping of the leaves, the garden inevitably goes into a green and brown phase. Traditionally, gardeners cheer things up by combining the red berries of the fishbone-branched *Cotoneaster horizontalis* with the yellow stars of winter jasmine on a sunny or shady wall. And here at home, I have added the November-flowering *Mahonia × media* 'Lionel Fortescue' ('Buckland' is better, I realized belatedly) to the border opposite the back door; the erect yellow sprays, 6 ft/2m up the woody branches (you can chop them back when they get too tall) are lit by the outdoor light. But even throwing in a spot of variegation and coloured dogwood stems, there isn't much to tickle the optic nerve.

So what about finding your colour from other sources? I wouldn't go as far as

← Previous page: Seedheads have long been an overlooked asset of perennials, but today's naturalistic borders are often planted specifically to develop into dried-flower arrangements for the winter months. *Phlomis russeliana* is one of the best contributors.

the gardeners I met in North Carolina, who spray-paint their herbaceous border in the autumn (a Gertrude Jekyll colour scheme – very tasteful). Nor as far as the TV gardeners who slosh the walls pink or blue.

But I have been inspired by Valerie Murray, who carries the terracotta walls and soft yellow window frames of her house in Victoria, British Columbia, out into the garden in the subtlest ways. In one small lawn, the colours are echoed in a pair of Adirondack-style garden seats painted lemon-white, and a solitary pot glazed yellow, simply stood in the empty border. The scene is part-screened by black-stemmed bamboo (*Phyllostachys nigra*).

But in front of the main door there is a big all-year scheme, with the adjacent garage doors painted in the contrasting livery of a large blue-grey and grey-green check, and all the colours picked up in a sea of evergreen pot plants, ranging from blue-green euphorbias and yuccas to yellow and bronze phormiums and old gold *Hebe ochracea*, interspersed with assorted objects like slim maple-syrup collecting tins in muted reds and oranges, and mustard-coloured plastic bowling balls (I'm not sure about them). It all adds up to an uplifting winter welcome.

MOVING THE SHOW INDOORS

Another remedy for floral deprivation outside is to pack the windowsills with colour. I love that contrast of warm, scented Riviera with the dark, drizzly Britain beyond the window. *Cymbidium* orchids bloom for ages, and are well worth the expense, even if you can't be bothered to grow them on from year to year. Forced hyacinths and potted crocuses are essential, as is an indoor jasmine. I give 'Paper White' narcissi a miss: they smell like the elephant house at Chester Zoo.

The white, lily-scented Maddenii rhododendrons have rather aristocratic associations, a fixture of stately home hallways, with the green Loden coat and Irish wolfhound. But if you have an airy, cold (but frost-free) glasshouse, conservatory or porch, you should indulge. My earliest and best, always out in

February, is an obscure one, *R. leucaspis × edgeworthii*, offered by the conservatory plant specialists Read's, of Loddon, Norfolk. Dense, compact, thriving on neglect, and yet smothered in white trumpets, mine has been going strong for years. 'Fragrantissimum' is the commonest variety, but it doesn't bloom until May.

PLANTING A WINTER GLADE

As the new year advances, outdoor flowers start appearing again in some numbers. Following my principle of grouping things together that bloom at the same time, I do suggest designating a couple of areas for a January to March splash. Inspired by Esther Merton, I dug out a strip of lawn under the outer canopy of my copper beech trees some eight years ago. A bed that is sunny in winter but shady in summer is ideal, since so many winter-flowering plants are woodlanders.

I structured it as a repeating pattern of evergreens – mostly green hollies at

the back, with a trio of variegated 'Golden King' hollies as a centrepiece, and alternating golden yews and lime-green Corsican hellebores along the front, to radiate a bit of warmth. That left me with three empty bays.

Into one of these I put a pair of witch-hazels, lemon *Hamamelis × intermedia* 'Pallida' and coppery-orange 'Jelena', which produce their spidery flowers simultaneously on bare branches in January. I would have added red 'Diane' if there had been space. ('Jelena' was raised by the great tree and shrub expert Madame Jelena de Belder in Belgium. On her engagement to her husband Robert, a wealthy diamond dealer, she asked if she could possibly have witch-hazels instead of diamonds as her present, and from these she did her hybridizing and selecting. Excellent priorities.) Into each of the other two bays I put a solitary pink daphne, February-flowering *D. bholua* and March-flowering *D. mezereum*.

The ground around them I then flushed with hellebores and bulbs – snowdrops, crocuses, pink and white hardy winter cyclamen (*C. coum*), 'February Gold' and white 'Jenny' daffodils, erythroniums and pale blue scillas. Most of the plants are freely mingled, though I keep the cyclamen close to the witch-hazels and daphnes, so they don't get drowned by beefy foliage.

Spaces between the bulbs I reserved for hostas and deciduous ferns, and these turn the bays into bands of contrasting leaf shapes for summer. The dormant rusty mounds of mature deciduous ferns are particularly good with yellow and cream spring bulbs, from winter aconites to daffodils. I realized this at Knightshayes, Devon, where the old *Polystichum* ferns stand in rivers of creamy-white erythroniums. With their oriental-looking bells, upturned at the tips, these are among my favourite woodland bulbs. Sulphur *Erythronium* 'Pagoda' and *E. californicum* 'White Beauty' are two of the best. I had a memorable afternoon in the Olympic Mountains, west of Seattle, watching white erythroniums emerging from the melting snow, being munched upon by deer.

The idea is that from the house you see the whole of my winter border through the flowering branches of a cherry, *Prunus subhirtella* 'Autumnalis Rosea', though this has been growing painfully slowly.

Since you can shop for most winter plants when they are in flower, there is

← | Even on a grim, overcast day, it is such a tonic wandering down to your winter glade to find out what is stirring.

instant gratification in planting a winter bed. And the continuing pleasure is that on those warm days, when the first bees are buzzing, it feels as if spring has arrived two months early, and you can be out there fiddling, adding something new, dividing the odd clump of snowdrops or crocuses as they are fading, or even in an emergency moving the odd hellebore in bloom (they don't mind when they are young, but are resentful of disturbance later). Nothing I have done in the garden has been more rewarding.

PATHWAY AMBUSHES FROM SCENTED SHRUBS

A large proportion of winter's shrubs are scented, and I like to reserve a few spaces for them close to the house, and along the garden's principal paths. That way, even when it is grey and drizzly and you are venturing out only to the garage, you get a morale-boosting blast.

The evergreen cushions of honey-scented Christmas box (*Sarcococca*) are ideal for path junctions. Some find the smell a little lavatorial, but it escapes mention in the cautionary German book I have just been given, *Der Stinkgarten*. The yellow streamers of *Mahonia japonica* (my mother's favourite

shrub) and the pink baubles of *Viburnum* × *bodnantense* 'Dawn' have more sophisticated flavours. Both have a long season, and can be good shrubs for the corners of front gardens, where fence meets pavement.

I am told that in Japan there are several hundred forms of Japanese apricot, *Prunus mume*, in cultivation, and yet mysteriously it is hardly known here. If you have room for a small tree, and can disguise its rather sickly-looking foliage in summer, then I strongly recommend the variety 'Beni-chidori'. The cloud of cerise-pink usually comes at the end of

February, and on warm days the rose perfume carries for yards. It blends well with blue-green conifers – and long-tailed tits, which strike me as very oriental-looking.

But if you can shoehorn in just one scented shrub, it should be *Daphne bholua* 'Jacqueline Postill'. This evergreen came into general circulation only a few years ago. The flowers – balls of pale pink stars from deep pink buds – start opening around New Year, last for a couple of months, and are extremely frost-proof (much more so than winter viburnum). It is vigorous and quickly makes a compact, upright plant 7ft/2.25m or so in height. Mine, in woodland glade conditions with plenty of leafmould in the soil, now stands in a little thicket of its own suckers.

I heard the story of its introduction after mentioning it in my newspaper column. It prompted a letter from a reader, Major Tom Spring-Smyth, who described walking in the Himalayas in the early sixties through groves of these daphnes flowering out of unspoilt snow, pumping the scent of fruit and spice into the air. He collected seedlings, which were sent off by Gurkha runner to British Gurkha HQ at Dharan, and thence via the diplomatic bag to Kew. It was a deciduous version that was raised at Kew, and it was called 'Gurkha' because, Major Spring-Smyth told me, 'it was tough like the Gurkha soldier'. 'Jacqueline Postill' is an evergreen seedling arising from 'Gurkha', and I think it has the edge over its parent.

LIVENING UP A SHADY WALL

One of the cosiest winter walls I have seen was on an old brick cottage in Hertfordshire. East-facing, I think, it was hidden under an overcoat of big-leaved variegated ivies, creamy 'Dentata Variegata' and the cheery yellow-splashed 'Sulphur Heart' ('Paddy's Pride'), framing the white windows.

In two places, a waterfall of grey catkins tumbled out of the ivy. These were provided by *Garrya elliptica* 'James Roof', one of the best evergreen shrubs for part shade (though it would rather have sun). For extra jollity, the owner could

← Left: *Prunus mume* 'Beni-chidori' forms a large, scruffy shrub, but the February colour and scent are sensational. It can suffer in very cold winters.

→ Next page: I rate *Daphne bholua* 'Jacqueline Postill' the best shrub introduction of recent years. Give it shelter, and a decently drained soil, and it ought to flourish in all but the coldest areas.

have planted the winter-flowering *Clematis cirrhosa* 'Freckles' to twine through its branches – giving the host a few years' head start. A bit of outdoor lighting also works wonders on garrya.

Daphne odora 'Aureomarginata', with fruitily scented purple and white stars, finds a place next to a shady wall in many a London garden, and gives good value over many weeks. But, like garrya, it prefers sunshine.

A HELLEBORE CORNER

Lenten roses, *Helleborus hybridus*, are a current craze, and a concentration of them in one section of shady border, or under a tree in the lawn, brings a carnival atmosphere for weeks. Nurserymen have taken their sweet time to realize the potential popularity of these early-flowering perennials, which come in such a range of colours and, for most people, are so easy to grow (though you may be forced to spray against blackspot).

But today, both the quantity and quality of plants in general circulation is so improved that you can afford to be really choosy. I like to pick out plants that

have strong colour on the reverse of their petals, or, in the case of the spotted sorts, have their flowers tilted slightly upwards so you don't have to bend down to see what they look like. But this problem is resolved if you can grow your hellebores on raised ground.

Visiting Susan Riley's garden in Victoria, Canada, I was impressed by a big drift of *Helleborus foetidus* Wester Flisk Group, with lime-green cups and red-flecked stems, around the trunk of a copper-brown paperbark maple. *H. foetidus* is a plant I have always taken rather for granted, letting it seed here and there in shady corners, but a deliberate mass of it is quite something.

LARGESSE WITH BULBS

Bulbs should certainly not be confined to your winter hot spots. All over the garden empty soil is crying out for them, and I am surprised more gardeners don't indulge. They can be spread around any deciduous tree or shrub, and even into the lawn or the perennial border, providing they are not among plants that have to be lifted or divided often. But you want them in splurges, not in dots.

Snowdrops are the prime candidates. The eye-opener for me was Bill Baker's little woodland beside the Thames (occasionally under the Thames) at Tidmarsh, Berkshire. His garden was a wonderland of white. Common snowdrops do like a bit of moisture in the soil, and if they aren't doing well, the remedy is almost certainly to transfer them to ground well-laced with leafmould or well-rotted compost. Dry dusty corners are hopeless.

It is well worth acquiring different sorts of snowdrop to extend the season. You can carry this to extreme lengths, as do the experts ('stamen-spotters' Mrs Merton called them) who assemble for 'snowdrop lunches' some time in February, to examine the intricacies of each other's collections with the aid of a hand lens, attempt identifications, and then propose swaps. Snowdrops being infinitely variable, a lifetime's pedantry is assured.

A few distinct and vigorous forms are all you really need. 'Atkinsii' opens

← Previous page: The dark Lenten roses, *Helleborus hybridus*, are particularly desirable, but need backlighting, such as from a drift of snowdrops, to show up well.

→ Right: Common snowdrops and yellow aconites, *Eranthis hyemalis*, need moisture in the soil if they are to luxuriate. It is easier to establish them as growing plants than as dry bulbs.

several weeks before the common snowdrop, is twice as tall, and clumps up quickly, while 'Lady Beatrix Stanley' is an elegant early double. Also in the vanguard are the snowdrops with broad grey leaves, like *Galanthus elwesii* – excellent in tandem with plum-coloured hellebores and white 'Jenny' daffodils – but they like full sun at flowering time. And with the main company of single and double common snowdrops comes 'Magnet', which swings its flowers as on fishing rods, and tall, buxom, strongly fragrant 'S. Arnott'.

Excellent partners for snowdrops are the leaves of the autumn-flowering hardy cyclamen, *C. hederifolium*, which carries its hummocks of patterned leaves through winter and spring. In Victoria Susan Riley has the two blended into a carpet, running down the entire narrow strip between her front drive and the fence – a fine treatment for an awkward site. They are also good against the marbled arrowhead foliage of *Arum italicum* 'Marmoratum' and the purplish hummocks of *Tellima grandiflora* Rubra Group – both stalwart woodland perennials.

The other winter bulb I like to let loose through swathes of border is the crocus, *C. tommasinianus*. This seeds and spreads very energetically, in sun or part shade, and comes in a range of tints from lilac to reddish-purple – enhanced, when the sun is out, by its dashing orange stigmata. It combines

particularly well with the hefty lime-green cups of Corsican hellebore, *Helleborus argutifolius*, which is one of my mainstay foreground evergreens, in both shade and sun.

COLOUR SPLASHES FOR OPEN SUNNY BORDERS

The very readable Edwardian garden writer E. A. Bowles ('The water is so hard here it would scarcely take a miracle to walk upon it') reckoned spring came to his Middlesex garden as early as September thanks to his generous plantings of sun-loving Algerian iris, *Iris unguicularis*. In my garden in the cooler north-west, it doesn't really get going until February at the earliest, but then I do get a generous crop of violet, scented flowers; purple in the case of 'Mary Barnard' and the dwarf 'Abington Purple'. Its cousin *I. lazica*, also violet, gives me a much longer season and clumps up much faster, but has broader and coarser leaves. Actually, all of them are a bit scruffy in their foliage, so if you decide to plant a run of them, I wouldn't make it anywhere too prominent.

Handsome companions for these winter irises are two knockout hybrid hellebores recently launched into general circulation, *Helleborus × nigercors* and *H. × ericsmithii*. Both are like big-flowered white Christmas roses, the former flushed yellow, the latter (which I prefer) marked in an array of apricot, plum and terracotta shades which are conspicuous for months. *H. × nigercors* I have backed by a blue evergreen *Euphorbia characias*; *H. × ericsmithii* by a purple evergreen 'Tom Thumb' pittosporum.

All are joined by sky-blue *Chionodoxa luciliae*, a starry-flowered bulb that seeds merrily along paving cracks and sunny border fringes. And in the background are the expanding white buds of the evergreen shrub *Osmanthus delavayi*.

Where sunny border drifts into woodland shade, I have a single plant of the shrubby Fuji cherry, *Prunus incisa* 'Kojo-no-mai', picking up the distant blossom of my big winter cherry. I wish I had planted three. Compact (and clippable),

and smothered in palest pink blossom (very showy against dark evergreens), the leaves are elegant enough not to be an embarrassment in summer. In autumn they turn orange-brown.

E. A. Bowles wrote that he took crocuses '*au grand sérieux*', and some of the *Crocus chrysanthus* cultivars and hybrids we grow today are of his raising. 'Cream Beauty', lavender 'Blue Pearl', 'Snow Bunting' and purple-striped 'Ladykiller' are all outstanding – rain permitting – and look well poking out of gravel, in front of evergreen shrubs like hebes ('evergrey' Mediterranean shrubs like lavender tend to look a bit bedraggled by late winter unless they have been clipped into tight ball shapes, as Marylyn Abbott does in her splendid potager at West Green House, Hampshire).

Clumps of compact, slow-developing perennials (such as *Sedum* 'Herbstfreude' and *Aster amellus* varieties) also make excellent companions for bulbs in sunny beds. If you plant the clumps a couple of feet apart, there is plenty of space between for a medley of small bulb species, beginning with crocuses and moving on to small daffodils and species tulips, scillas and muscari.

I find another very good place for colonies of these early dwarf bulbs to be the front strip of a border, which I can mentally designate as bulb territory and so remember not to spear with a fork; there are merits, too, in having all the

↑ Algerian iris, *Iris unguicularis* (*left*), produces an unexpectedly sumptuous flower for the time of year. *Prunus incisa* (*right*), here in its form 'Kojo-no-mai', gives 'the first bee concert of spring'.

scruffiness of the dying bulb leaves concentrated in the foreground beside the lawn, which the eye can just pass over as if it were a strip of rough grass.

EARLY MARCH BLUES

Intense blue is a rare colour in hardy plants, and there is an unmissable opportunity in this late winter-spring period to ladle it about. Among bulbs, gentian-blue *Scilla siberica* 'Spring Beauty' is the most electrifying, and thrives in both sun and part shade. I have it in my woodland areas both on its own, in pools between evergreens like shiny green *Sarcococca confusa* and golden yew, and combined with 'February Gold' daffodils.

On sunny gravel, I grow it with white, dome-flowered *Bergenia* 'Beethoven' and the bicoloured navy and mid-blue grape hyacinth *Muscari latifolium*. This is well partnered in the Savill Garden, Windsor, with the sprawling *Euphorbia myrsinites*, which has blue-green, rather reptilian foliage and lime-green flowerheads.

Among perennials, the prime sources of late winter blues are the shade- and moisture-loving lungworts. *Pulmonaria* 'Frühlingshimmel' is one of a number

of sky-blues, 'Mawson's Variety' one of a number of royal blues. I let yellow violets and Bowles' golden grass (*Milium effusum* 'Aureum') seed about them; this grass looks particularly good beside those pulmonarias with silver-spotted leaves. Over one of my groups presides *Stachyurus* 'Magpie', which hangs straw-yellow tassels from red-brown stems in March, and follows up with white-splashed leaves for summer.

OTHER EXCELLENT WINTER-FLOWERING PLANTS

woodland glades

SHRUBS

- Camellia × williamsii 'J. C. Williams'
- Corylopsis glabrescens
- Corylus avellana
- Lonicera × purpusii
- Rhododendron lutescens
- Rhododendron 'Praecox'
- Ribes sanguineum 'White Icicle'
- Viburnum tinus 'Eve Price'
- Viburnum tinus 'Gwenllian'

PERENNIALS

Pulmonaria rubra

Viola odorata

gravel and terrace

WALL SHRUBS

- Azara microphylla
- Chimonanthus praecox

Bergenia × schmidtii

← This is the moment for a splurge of blue and yellow: here, *Narcissus* 'Tête à Tête' and *Scilla siberica* 'Spring Beauty'.

8 — SPRING

Some time in March, the garden's woody backbone starts to break out in leaf and flower. Give me a few days of sun, when the bronze leaves and white blossom of wild cherry and amelanchier are out, and my sunny border's principal evergreens – *Viburnum* × *burkwoodii* and *Osmanthus delavayi* – are wafting spicy scent across the emerging daylily and peony leaves, and it takes wild horses (or at least a seriously agitated phone-call from an editor, wondering why my article hasn't arrived) to drag me out of the garden to the dreaded computer.

MORE LARGESSE WITH BULBS

The taller daffodils are plants for massing in grass, around orchard trees (white daffs under white cherries, for instance), and towards the back of borders, where the conspicuous sheaves of long leaves have a chance of being lost as they are dying. I prefer the soft yellows and creamy whites to the brassier varieties, but all have their role (excluding the squashed-nose monstrosities concocted by modern breeders). And with the pheasant-eye types like 'Actaea', scented whites with a small orange cup, the season extends well into May. There is a memorable drift of them at Lanhydrock, Bodmin, backed by flashes of blood-red rhododendron.

← Previous page: Empty ground under deciduous trees and shrubs is ground wasted. Here at The Garden House, the spring carpet comprises yellow *Erythronium* 'Pagoda' and blue *Corydalis flexuosa*.

← Left: The blossom of a magnolia illuminates a shady path at The Garden House.

The other tribe of bulbs to take seriously is the anemones. White *A. nemorosa*, which is wild in the oak woods a mile from me, is a vigorous colonizer, but since it disappears discreetly in summer that is seldom a worry. The blues and whites of *A. blanda* and the taller *A. apennina* can be flushed through any sunny or part-shaded corner; they are great together, among the red leaves of ornamental rhubarb, *Rheum palmatum* 'Bowles' Red', and emerging herbaceous and tree peonies (my favourite partners for spring bulbs) and as companions to yellow daffodils. There is a tremendous show of them at Highdown, Goring-on-Sea.

A potential complication in adding spring bulbs to borders is the fact that most of them are sold only in the autumn. The garden looks completely different then, you have forgotten where you want them, and wherever you plunge a spade into the ground, there is a heart-stopping scrunch as you strike bulbs already in situ.

I came upon the solution (at least for small-scale bulb planting) at Sissinghurst. In autumn, you plant your bulbs shallowly in pots, which you plunge to the correct depth in rows somewhere out of the way, say under the soil of the vegetable patch. As they come into bloom, you lift the pots, transport them to the border, dig a hole, gingerly remove the pots, and slip in the bulbs.

POND LIFE

The early spring spectacle of a hundred or more slimy black frogs in my pond, burping and writhing in pairs, soon cures visiting children of storybook notions of frogs as green, musical creatures, poised to transmogrify into princes. I try to dredge the pond of weed before their arrival, to avoid the hazard of frogspawn. In April, the tadpoles are hatched.

The creamy white version of marsh marigold, *Caltha palustris* var. *alba*, nestling among the water iris leaves, is a handsome perennial with which to kickstart the pondside's flowering year; the single white bamboo-like kerria

blooms at the same time and echoes it perfectly. Soon afterwards, the yellow spathes of the skunk cabbage, *Lysichiton americanus*, start appearing. The smell is absolutely disgusting at first, but eventually mellows into a sour pong; the white *L. camtschatcensis* does not have this defect, and can be allowed in the foreground.

I like to make the most of the young foliage now appearing in the nearby border – coppery astilbe, purplish ligularia, bronze rodgersia – by interplanting with the giant white snowdrop-like snowflake, *Leucojum aestivum* 'Gravetye Giant' (and, in the moister spots, with the lavender drumstick primula, *P. denticulata*).

Other candidates – all of which also look good in short spring grass beside water – are hoop-petticoat daffodils (*Narcissus bulbocodium* var. *citrinus*), primroses, cowslips, lady's smock (*Cardamine pratensis*), and the chequered

↑ A patch of lawn is the ideal spot for a show of snakeshead fritillaries, *Fritillaria meleagris*, which naturalize readily given sufficient moisture.

belled snakeshead fritillary, *Fritillaria meleagris* – the most mesmerizing spring bulb of the lot. Anyone who has not seen a water meadow stained purple with fritillaries should visit Magdalen College, Oxford, in late April or early May. Annoyingly, the river bank is too high for them to be viewed while punting, so you must take a walk first. In a part-shaded border, the snakeshead fritillary combines well with anemones and sky-blue pulmonarias.

TULIPS IN CONTAINERS

Unlike daffodils, tulips are unpredictable in the border. Some persist happily from year to year, others dwindle and disappear. Deep planting (8 inches/20cm or more) seems to encourage longevity, but you can't rely on it. So recently I have been growing most of my tulips in containers (again, easier to plant in autumn), which I mass between the old 'Sissinghurst Blue' rosemary on the terrace and the trunk of my paperbark maple.

Over the years I have picked up a few copper laundry basins from bric-à-brac shops and, inspired by Sissinghurst, I plant them with short, blue-leaved

tulips, deep red 'Couleur Cardinal' and orange 'Prinses Irene', interplanted with *Scilla* 'Spring Beauty', which starts the show a month earlier. My other stalwarts are scarlet 'Red Georgette' and 'Red Shine', mahogany and orange 'Abu Hassan' and 'Queen of Sheba', damson 'Queen of Night' and the crinkly-edged parrot tulips 'Black Parrot', 'Flaming Parrot' . . . I wonder when they will bring out 'Sick as a Parrot'.

SUNNY WALLS AND TERRACES

The sunny border beside Barbara Joseph's terrace lawn, near Welshpool, conveys the excitement of spring with a whoosh of hot colours. It is a real tonic. The mainstay along the back row is several plants of the tall evergreen *Berberis darwinii*, with bright orange blossom.

In between is the shrubby Madeiran euphorbia, *E. mellifera*, whose honey-brown, honey-scented flowers (which have a powerful attraction for ants) appear above exotic, emerald-green leaves; it needs a warm wall outside the milder counties. Where an apple tree casts dappled shade, golden philadelphus glows in its new lemon-yellow livery. And along the front row are golden grasses and the herbaceous euphorbia *E. polychroma*, whose lime-yellow flowerheads are among the most dazzling of its tribe. Scarlet tulips are thrown in for good measure.

She might also have used yellow and orange crown imperials, *Fritillaria imperialis*, a bulb whose giant bells, topped by a pineapple-like tuft, are another highlight of April (they are also effective standing alone, waking up an otherwise empty herbaceous border). As a backing to crown imperials and orange berberis in my garden, I use the coppery leaves of amelanchier.

A quieter approach has been taken along the elegant brick terraces and against the pale, pebble-dashed walls at Les Moutiers, a house (rather grim) designed by Lutyens on an exposed ridge near Dieppe. Pale pink *Clematis montana* dripping from the walls and billowing thunderclouds of dark blue blossom from the evergreen *Ceanothus* 'Puget Blue' (one of the best of all wall

← Previous page: Tulips are made for containers. Around my stone steps (*right*) I partner them with pots of tender, scented Maddenii rhododendrons, including 'Fragrantissimum', 'Lady Alice Fitzwilliam', and (*left*) 'Countess of Haddington', seen here between the tulips 'Red Shine' and 'Queen of Night'.

shrubs) provide the spring backdrop. The borders are formally structured with yew topiaries and repeated clumps of silver-leaved perennials like stachys and artemisia. And here and there a large shimmering silver shrub of *Elaeagnus commutata* gives a focal point.

At ground level the colour comes from mixed plum and white tulips, mats of the evergreen perennial *Iberis sempervirens*, which is now a dome of white, lime-green *Euphorbia characias* subsp. *wulfenii*, and blue rosemaries. All very restrained. I don't think I could have resisted weaving in a few seasonal blood-red wall shrubs – an ornamental quince like *Chaenomeles* × *superba* 'Rowallane' or the fuchsia-like flowering currant *Ribes speciosum* – which look so good with rosemary and ceanothus.

One other evergreen which I don't remember seeing at Les Moutiers but which would have slotted in well is the perennial wallflower *Erysimum* 'Bowles' Mauve'. It is not long-lived, but since it blooms pretty much the entire year, it gives good value. It combines well not only with plum tulips but with purple sage, self-seeding *Viola* 'Bowles' Black', the white, purple-backed daisies of osteospermum and, later, that outstanding (and self-supporting) short black iris, 'Langport Wren'.

For scent, the finishing touch to all planting schemes, I would have added the perennial stock *Matthiola incana* 'White Perennial'. The grey rosettes seed themselves into paving cracks, and, come April, a heavy clove fragrance travels on the evening air.

WOODLAND BLUES

The surge of blue bulbs and woodland perennials continues, now including forget-me-nots and English and taller Spanish bluebells. Another plant that seeds generously along shady paving cracks is *Brunnera macrophylla*, which resembles a forget-me-not in flower but has oval leaves (the cultivar called 'Langtrees', with grey flecks on its foliage, also pops up, true to type).

All these plants are blended into a memorable scene in architect Peter

Aldington's garden at Haddenham, in Buckinghamshire. The house is post-war, of imaginative design – a rare item, thanks to our stultified planning regulations.

From the back door, you step out into a small glade formed by pale-trunked birches, a haze of blues mixed with the whites and greens of anemones, Solomon's seal (*Polygonatum*), tellima, *Euphorbia amygdaloides* var. *robbiae* and, in the distance, Mexican orange blossom (*Choisya*) – a tiered *Viburnum plicatum* 'Mariesii' would also have worked well as an eyecatcher. I remember ground-hugging blue ajuga and blue-white *Phlox divaricata* in tandem, and to spice things up there were red aquilegias and a few bright yellows from Welsh poppies (a dangerous seeder), and, on the sunny fringe, the shrub rose 'Frühlingsgold'.

He might also have exploited the brilliant new leaves of golden philadelphus and golden elder. Other pairings I could have suggested, gleaned from my travels, are shuttlecock ferns (*Matteuccia*) spearing through mats of white-plumed *Tiarella cordifolia*; the brick-red perennial *Geum rivale* 'Leonard's Variety' with *Geranium macrorrhizum* 'Album'; alchemilla and golden berberis; and, of course, wild primroses and violets.

To extend the colour to shady walls, you could look to the spring-flowering clematis. *C. montana* is a vigorous brute, and requires a large expanse of wall or shed roof (or host tree). But *C. alpina* 'Frances Rivis', with violet-blue bells, is altogether more delicate. I have it twining through the pale yellow-funnelled deciduous shrub *Weigela middendorffiana*.

RHODODENDRON HEAVEN

Prejudices are essential when you start out as a gardener, otherwise you haven't a hope of charting a course through the world's flora. But since they are

↑ The less vigorous climbers, such as *Clematis alpina*, can be let loose around the garden. Yellow *Weigela middendorffiana* was my father's favourite shrub.

→ Visitors often mistake *Rhododendron trichostomum* for a daphne. It is small, has a spicy scent, and is far removed from the popular image of a rhodo as a blowsy lump.

invariably based on ignorance, sooner or later you are bound to be jolted into a volte-face. So it was with me and rhododendrons. The name simply conjured up visions of dolled-up hillocks as subtle as a Barbara Cartland frock. Then I spent one spring among the woodland gardens of Devon and Cornwall and realized my mistake. All those years wasted.

Deciduous azaleas are tasteful enough even to find their way through the gates of Sissinghurst. The common azalea, *Rhododendron luteum*, with its soft yellow trumpets and honeysuckle scent, and leaves flaring up in the autumn, is still hard to beat, especially in a carpet of bluebells. The Ghent hybrid 'Narcissiflorum' has the same colour flowers, attractively semi-double, on a more compact plant; 'Daviesii' is a handsome white. If you don't have acid soil, they grow well in half-barrels along a part-shaded path.

In smaller gardens, it is hard to justify evergreen rhodos in groups, because most are such dull lumps after flowering. They need to be integrated with other shrubs on the fringes of borders. Among the shorter varieties, I like scarlet 'May Day' (resistant to mildew, unlike the similar 'Elizabeth', and good behind *Skimmia × confusa* 'Kew Green') and the thimble-flowered pink *R. trichostomum* and its white hybrid 'Arctic Tern' – ideal rhodos with which to test the prejudices of friends, because they look just like daphnes. *R. augustinii* 'Electra' is a tall violet-blue, *R. wardii* a compact primrose-yellow.

Among the whoppers, 'Sir Charles Lemon' is splendid, with cinnamon undersides to its leaves and, eventually, white flowers; 'Loder's White' is a more reliable bloomer, even on dryish soil. But my favourites are the elephantine-leaved *R. macabeanum*, and *R.* 'Loderi King George', which exhales lily scent from large, pink-flushed white trumpets.

With their dense rootballs and low, dense canopies, rhodos are not sociable towards companion perennials, and as my plants grow I am forever rescuing the shrinking violets underneath. Bluebells, forget-me-nots and self-sporing ferns are more expendable.

MOSSY TROUGHS IN SHADY CORNERS

So many of the small jewel-like woodlanders out now are rather wasted at ground level. Also, many of them prefer a moist, well-drained fibrous acid soil which you may not naturally be able to provide. The answer is a raised bed or a deep stone trough.

Prime candidates are the painted fern, *Athyrium niponicum* var. *pictum*, starry white *Epimedium* × *youngianum* 'Niveum', pale blue *Jeffersonia dubia*, and sulphur-yellow *Uvularia grandiflora* var. *pallida* (if you've got acid soil, this is excellent out in the border with *Omphalodes cappadocica* 'Cherry Ingram', one of the most intense blue perennials of the season).

Some plants deserve a trough to themselves. I remember one devoted to the sky-blue Virginian cowslip, *Mertensia pulmonarioides* (syn. *M. virginica*), in Penelope Hobhouse's Dorset garden. And here at home I have one reserved for the double white bloodroot, *Sanguinaria canadensis* 'Plena', whose flowers, like miniature waterlilies, are among the most beautiful of the year. They are fleeting, but no doubt that's why I value them so much.

Somewhere, I read a story of a man being taken to a house up a mountain to see the finest view in all Japan. During tea the screens were kept firmly shut, and only as he was about to leave were they drawn back for a moment. The pleasure was concentrated and intensified. Very Japanese. Back home in the

← | I choose my rhodos as much for their scent as for their colour. Here, an unnamed deciduous azalea hybrid, fringed by *Omphalodes cappadocica* (*left*), and R. 'Loderi King George' (*right*) bloom along the shady edge of my lawn.

garden, you need plants that bloom on and on, but you also need plants that fill you with anticipation, perform memorably, and then vanish before you have time to take them for granted.

HOSTAS IN SHADY BEDS AND CONTAINERS

Most hostas are at their best in May, slugs permitting. My recipe is a lacing of sharp grit and a slug-killer based on aluminium sulphate (reputedly harmless to other wildlife) applied tight around the base of the plants. I choose dry days, scatter the granules weekly during April, May and June, then hand over the job to the mistle-thrushes and frogs.

My Canadian friend Terri Clark alternates hostas with maidenhair ferns (*Adiantum pedatum*) along one shady pathway. Hostas and ferns are a terrific team, and since there is so much variety among them, you can keep the planting interesting for yards. At Lady Farm, Judy Pearce interplants her hostas with the tall pink ornamental onion *Allium hollandicum* and its darker cultivar 'Purple Sensation', which do surprisingly well in dappled shade.

Of the plants you can grow in summer containers in shady spots, hostas are among the best (with fuchsias, hydrangeas and busy lizzies). I have an enormous blue-and-yellow-leaved 'Frances Williams' growing out of a half-barrel in the north-facing yard by the back door.

AWAKENING MEADOW PERENNIALS

Daffodils and other bulbs give the meadow border most of its early colour. By May, *Camassia leichtlinii* subsp. *suksdorfii*, with violet-blue stars on 18 inch/ 45cm stems, is out ('Electra' is a good cultivar). Purples and blues show up well between all the fresh green mounds of rising foliage. A little later, Judy Pearce achieves the same effect at Lady Farm, using clumps of *Salvia × sylvestris*

← Left: 'June' is a gem of a hosta, with medium-sized leaves. It looks good in front of yellow azaleas.

→ Next page: It takes around four years for self-sown seed of *Tulipa sprengeri* to mature into flowering-sized bulbs, but the resulting sheet of red is worth waiting for.

'Mainacht' and *Geranium ibericum* dotted through her late-flowering prairie perennials (heleniums, rudbeckias, echinaceas and the like).

But there are now enough flowering perennials to make a lively scene in many a cottage garden. At The Old Chapel, Chalford, Fiona Owen has planted a medley up the side of her hillside, with black, pink and white aquilegias, the fluffy lilac heads of meadow rue, *Thalictrum aquilegiifolium* ('Thundercloud' is a more saturated form), and the white and pink of self-seeding sweet rocket, *Hesperis matronalis*. Shrub roses perform later.

Aquilegias are a mixed blessing in borders, interbreeding shamelessly and seeding themselves where their fat roots are hard to extract. But they have great charm, from the ordinary sorts sprouting among the bluebells and forget-me-nots, to the more sophisticated doubles and bicolours like purple and white 'William Guinness'.

STUDY IN SCARLET

One of the most talented and formidable gardeners I have known was the late Netta Statham, who gardened on the Shropshire border. Forty years living in England had done nothing to soften her largely impenetrable Fife accent, or her

sharp tongue. There were no grey areas in her world. A plant was wonderful or it was 'rubbish', someone was a great friend or in her 'bad books' – 'And once in, you never get out,' she confided in me once.

There was no pussy-footing around the pastels in her immaculately presented acre, stuffed with rarities and her own seed-raised selections. In late spring, the place turned scarlet and lime-green. The oriental poppy *Papaver orientale* 'Beauty of Livermere' – a true blood-red, not orange – was a principal contributor, several clumps of it standing proud amid the green foliage of later-flowering perennials (it plays a similar solo act at Powis Castle, backed by *Ceanothus* 'Puget Blue').

All around, quite literally in sheets, seeding through sunny and part-shaded border, peat beds and gravel paths, was the tulip *T. sprengeri*. One of the last of its tribe to open, with slim pointed flowers in guardsman's red, this is the only tulip guaranteed to colonize in any garden. It has never been common in the nursery trade, but you should accept the heavy price tag, buy a few, and watch your investment grow. Here at home, I have it seeding around the primrose-yellow shrub rose *R.* 'Cantabrigiensis'. Netta had it among limy *Smyrnium perfoliatum* and euphorbias.

OTHER EXCELLENT SPRING-FLOWERING PLANTS

gravel and terrace	meadow borders	woodland glades
SHRUBS		
◊ *Cytisus* × *kewensis*		◊ *Magnolia stellata*
◊ *Cytisus* × *praecox*		✦ *Mahonia* × *wagneri*
◊ *Daphne* × *burkwoodii*		✦ *Pieris* 'Forest Flame'
'Somerset'		✦ *Pieris formosa* var. *forrestii*
✦ *Daphne tangutica*		'Wakehurst'
✦ *Erica arborea* 'Alpina'		✦ *Pieris* 'Grayswood'
✦ *Osmanthus delavayi*		◊ *Rhododendron vaseyi*
◊ *Paeonia delavayi*		✦ *Skimmia japonica* 'Rubella'
◊ *Paeonia delavayi* var.		◊ *Viburnum* × *juddii*
ludlowii		
◊ *Potentilla fruticosa*		
'Abbotswood'		
◊ *Rosa pimpinellifolia*		
'Double White'		
✦ *Rosmarinus officinalis*		
Prostratus Group		
◊ *Spiraea* 'Arguta'		
CLIMBERS		
✦ *Clematis armandii*		
◊ *Eccremocarpus scaber*		
◊ *Rosa banksiae* 'Lutea'		

←   Previous page: Oriental poppies are excellent stand-alone plants for waking up summer borders, and you can chop them to the ground after flowering. I am not sure if this is 'Beauty of Livermere' or 'Goliath'; they are almost identical.

gravel and terrace	meadow borders	woodland glades

PERENNIALS

Anemone fulgens	*Muscari armeniacum*	*Convallaria majalis*
Anthemis punctata subsp.	*Narcissus jonquilla*	*Corydalis flexuosa*
cupaniana	*Primula* (*Polyanthus*)	*Dicentra* 'Bacchanal'
Asphodeline lutea	*Trollius* × *cultorum*	*Doronicum* 'Miss Mason'
Aurinia saxatilis 'Citrina' (syn.	'Alabaster'	*Epimedium* × *rubrum*
Alyssum saxatile	*Trollius* × *cultorum*	*Epimedium* × *versicolor*
'Citrinum')	'Superbus'	'Sulphureum'
Iris (dwarf bearded)		*Lathyrus vernus* 'Roseus'
Iris 'Tinkerbell'		*Lunaria annua*
Lithodora diffusa 'Grace		*Lunaria rediviva*
Ward'		*Smilacina racemosa*
Narcissus minor		*Trillium*
Narcissus 'W. P. Milner'		
Pulsatilla vulgaris rubra		
Tulipa clusiana var.		
chrysantha		
Tulipa orphanidea		

9 — EARLY-MID SUMMER

This is the climax for many people. The trees are in new leaf, the borders have filled out, and a tidal wave of flower is crashing over gardens. Restraint is hard, but when this May–July period passes, you don't want your floral year to end with it. So try not to use up all the best sunny spots, or to make concentrations of plants that look a shambles after flowering. Easier said than done, I know.

WARM WALLS

Walking through London in May, I make the odd detour to look at the Chinese wisterias, *W. sinensis*, in the smarter Kensington squares. They are terrific with the pristine white paintwork, the black railings, and the gleaming BMW 7 Series. Drinking in the smell, I ponder where I have gone wrong in my ascent up the property ladder (not buying in Notting Hill five years ago, that's where).

The Japanese *W. floribunda* 'Multijuga' (syn. *W. f.* 'Macrobotrys'), which has the longest racemes and blooms after its leaves have emerged, is the cultivar I inherited on the south wall at home. Inspired by the terraces at Powis Castle, I partner it with the tall, erect shrub *Abutilon vitifolium* 'Tennant's White', whose huge white saucers and vine-like leaves look too exotic to be hardy, but are in fact extremely so – though plants do wear themselves out, and need replacing every five years.

On the basis that a trio of different elements is twice as pleasing as a duo, I have also added the mid-height sky-blue evergreen *Ceanothus* 'Southmead'.

Powis has a seventeenth-century lead shepherdess as its third item – stolen in a daring night raid some years ago, with the aid of a crane, but fortunately soon recovered; the statues are now alarmed.

MEDITERRANEAN TERRACES

The flavour of southern France or Italy is now yours for the taking, as the first and best of the tall bearded irises, pale blue *Iris pallida*, comes into flower. A pity we don't get the accompanying song of nightingales. This iris keeps good grey fans of leaves through the summer, while its hybrid cousins sear and shrivel, but in all cases the best recipe is to interplant with summer-flowering bulbs like Californian *Triteleia laxa* 'Konigin Fabiola', with starry blue heads, or *Allium christophii*, with large mauve globes and then parchment seedheads.

This is the beginning of peak season for communities of grey-green Mediterranean shrubs, which are now fully recovered from the wet winter and bristling with new leaves and flower-buds.

Rock roses are fine evergreens to build a planting around, especially *Cistus* × *cyprius*, with maroon-blotched white saucers and dark metallic leaves, and the intense pink *C.* × *purpureus*. This last holds court on the well-drained Aviary Terrace at Powis Castle, among silver-leaved artemisias, rose-pink diascias and spent iris foliage. The tall stems and wispy pale pink rockets of *Linaria purpurea* 'Canon Went', dotted here and there, lend a casual air.

A very attractive look can be had from all these low and mid-height hummocky shrubs – ripples of green cistus, grey *Phlomis fruticosa*, blue-green euphorbia, sages, lavenders, even purple berberis – interrupted by bands of tall

slim bulbs like *Allium hollandicum* or magenta *Gladiolus communis* subsp. *byzantinus*, or the yellow spikes of verbascums. I like the partnership at Kiftsgate, Gloucestershire, of *Allium christophii* with the silver leaves and emerging cream buds of cotton lavender, *Santolina pinnata* subsp. *neapolitana*.

At Upton House, near Banbury, the cotton lavender is seen through a mass of red valerian, *Centranthus ruber*, self-sown in the dry stone walls. This is a great plant to let loose through terrace paving cracks (together with Mexican daisy, *Erigeron karvinskianus*), flowering repeatedly – the proviso being that you curb its colonizing ambitions, when you have enough of it, by selective removal of its seedheads. Its white version sprouts between mounds of grey lavender along the honey-coloured walls of Hestercombe, Somerset, a Gertrude Jekyll garden for a long time managed by the Somerset Fire Brigade in between emergencies.

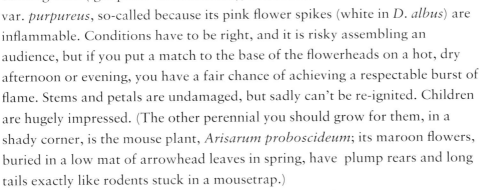

The most entertaining Mediterranean perennial is the burning bush ('gas plant' to Americans), *Dictamnus albus* var. *purpureus*, so-called because its pink flower spikes (white in *D. albus*) are inflammable. Conditions have to be right, and it is risky assembling an audience, but if you put a match to the base of the flowerheads on a hot, dry afternoon or evening, you have a fair chance of achieving a respectable burst of flame. Stems and petals are undamaged, but sadly can't be re-ignited. Children are hugely impressed. (The other perennial you should grow for them, in a shady corner, is the mouse plant, *Arisarum proboscideum*; its maroon flowers, buried in a low mat of arrowhead leaves in spring, have plump rears and long tails exactly like rodents stuck in a mousetrap.)

Brassy yellow brooms, like short *Genista lydia*, tall Spanish broom, *Spartium junceum*, and tree-like Mount Etna broom, *G. aetnensis*, add spice to such pinky schemes, as well as contrast in habit. And if there is a warm wall handy, Moroccan broom, *Cytisus battandieri*, makes an effective silvery feature, studded with yellow cones, scented of pineapple. It can be grown out in the open, but takes up a huge amount of space, which is hard to justify. It is well partnered in the Tindleys' London garden with the white-flowered climber *Solanum jasminoides* 'Album', which blooms almost

← *Cistus* × *cyprius* is one of the hardier rock roses.
↑ Clove-scented stock, *Matthiola incana* 'White Perennial', seeds itself into the cracks of my narrow terrace path, below the wall shrub *Solanum crispum* 'Glasnevin'.

continually from midsummer to late autumn. Away from mild climates, it is less reliable.

A MEDLEY OF 'STEPPE' PERENNIALS FOR SUNNY WELL-DRAINED SOIL

'Let's go wild like the Germans' was the excellent heading dreamed up by the *Telegraph* sub-editors for my first article on new-wave German planting, following a visit to the Stuttgart Garden Festival in 1993. There I was introduced to the naturalistic style of arranging perennials not in segregated clumps but in broken drifts and tufts, freely mingled, and with each variety repeated again and again through a matrix of ornamental grasses.

The prime showcase was a long, steep slope on sunny, well-drained soil, given over to loose bands of grey catmint and lavender, and a wide range of hardy, purple-spiked salvias, like *S. nemorosa* 'Ostfriesland', *S. × sylvestris* 'Mainacht' and blue *S. × s.* 'Blauhügel'. These were the theme plants, and between them were perennials of contrasting shapes and colours: the white and carmine-red discs of *Lychnis coronaria*, the crimson pincushions of *Knautia macedonica* (outstanding in tandem with salvias), and the yellow spires of verbascums. In one spot, the salvias meandered through the flat yellow plates of *Achillea* 'Coronation Gold'.

Since then, I have seen many equally appealing scenes in Germany using a similar range of early summer plants. Between the salvias and catmint, some designers weave in slabs of *Phlomis russeliana*, with whorls of creamy-yellow flowers up its tall stems, or bulbs like wine-purple *Allium sphaerocephalon* and starry white St Bernard's lily, *Anthericum liliago*. Occasionally, the planting descends on to prostrate rugs of thymes.

Among the grasses used are blue-leaved *Helictotrichon sempervirens*, *Stipa calamagrostis*, which has fluffy parchment plumes in July, and the giant oat grass, *Stipa gigantea*. And often the season is extended with the likes of short irises and yellow asphodels for May, and lavenders, *Sedum* 'Herbstfreude', violet-blue *Aster* × *frikartii* 'Mönch', and European mountain asters, *A. amellus* cultivars, for later. As a silvery foliage plant, I noted *Artemisia pontica* a splendid partner for both salvias and sedum.

At Lady Farm, Judy Pearce goes for a richer colour scheme, incorporating plenty of warm tinted irises, acid-yellow euphorbias, bronze *Carex* sedges, and orange pokers (*Kniphofia*). Later in the summer come intense-blue sea hollies (*Eryngium*) and the golden daisies of *Coreopsis verticillata*. Feathery cream *Stipa tenuissima* grass provides constant movement, and its bleached flowerheads last deep into the winter.

ROSE TIME

There has been a huge swing away from the sort of roses my grandparents loved, fancy Hybrid Teas and Floribundas with names like 'Tallyho' and 'Gay Gordons'. In summer, borders glowed like Las Vegas, in winter they looked like the Somme.

But even among the wild species and simpler hybrids – the easiest roses to incorporate into naturalistic scenes – very few stand up to scrutiny after their flowering moment is over. So I think of roses as plants for the fringes of a garden, where you can more easily distract attention from them.

Most shrub roses fit in well with the sort of dry habitat plantings I have described above. Forms of Scotch briar, like single white *Rosa pimpinellifolia* 'Grandiflora' (syn. *R. p.* 'Altaica'), and its elegant pink and white doubles, make neat bushes, clad in ferny leaves and, after flowering, numerous round chestnut-black hips. Blush-pink 'Stanwell Perpetual' blooms all summer. And I am very fond of the semi-double, lilac-pink *R. nutkana* 'Plena', though it takes up a lot of space and flowers only once. Likewise, 'Cerise Bouquet', one of the most eyecatching of all roses in its moment of glory – absolutely electrifying on the grass orchard bank at Powis Castle, with ox-eye daisies.

Like Scotch briar, Japanese roses, *R. rugosa*, are found wild on sand dunes. These are very good-value shrubs for the back of well-drained borders, those

with single white, crimson, or mauve-pink flowers following up with generous crops of red, tomato-shaped hips, while the double-flowered forms bloom continuously all summer, the fragrance travelling far. What's more, the leaves often turn a bright gold in the autumn.

Their hybrid 'Agnes' has few of these qualities, but I have a soft spot for it on account of the delectable amber-yellow colouring of its semi-double flowers, produced as early as mid-May, and its potent scent. I wore it as a buttonhole at the wedding of my friends Jonathan and Gillie Shaw, and, I kid you not, hatted heads were turning two pews in front of me as they picked up the lemon vapour trails. In their garden in Normandy, the Shaws have teamed up 'Agnes' very successfully with blue irises, purple bumble-bee-like French lavender (*Lavandula stoechas*), white daisy-flowered osteospermum, and violet Japanese wisteria. For more soft yellow, they could have added the iris-like fans of *Sisyrinchium striatum*.

Against a hot wall (though growing roses on any wall is to court mildew and blackspot; they are much better with free air circulation), I don't think you can beat the China roses, which bloom from early summer often until Christmas. For me, the semi-double pink 'Old Blush' and the extraordinary 'Mutabilis', whose flowers turn from apricot to pink to crimson as they age, are the prime contenders. They make good shrubs, but against walls they ascend to 8ft/2.5m or so. As a 2ft/60cm bush, pale pink 'Cécile Brünner' is a non-stop gem; 'Bloomfield Abundance' is a taller version: both are splendid out in the open.

The giant rambler roses have to be approached with caution. I heard of someone who planted a 'Kiftsgate' on each corner of a small summerhouse. You would not want to be sitting in that a few years down the line. The parent plant at Kiftsgate was at least 80ft/25m across and 30ft/9m high the last time I looked. But all gardens need moments of utter exuberance, and these monsters

↑ Rosa 'Agnes' starts flowering in May, and usually comes to the Chelsea Flower Show in my buttonhole.

really are one of the spectacles of the floral year, an explosion of scented white or pink blossom in early July, and later orange hips. Esther Merton specialized in them, the outhouses, old trees and dividing walls buried in petals (you don't want to plant big ramblers anywhere you have to train or prune them regularly – best just to let them get on with it). The trouble was that you could never find out what any of them were, since she simply named them after the place she had gleaned the cuttings: 'Burghfield Bus Stop', for instance.

At Millgate House, in the centre of Richmond, Yorkshire, the superb *Rosa helenae* – equal in beauty to 'Kiftsgate' but not quite as vigorous – grows up a reinforced iron pergola in the lawn, the centrepiece to one of the loveliest shrub rose gardens in Britain. Sadly, I haven't room at home for anything of this size, so I stick with the more modest amber-white 'Goldfinch', pinky-white 'Francis E. Lester' (reliable with its crop of orange hips), and purplish-crimson 'Veilchenblau' up my apple trees. Other excellent once-flowering ramblers are 'The Garland', in white, and 'Albertine' in coppery-pink.

SOPHISTICATED ROSES

Let's not pretend that the petal-packed shrub roses of the medieval troubadours and seventeenth-century Dutch painters are ideal garden plants. They contribute nothing for forty-six weeks of the year, and if we get a wet spell in June, the flowers are a write-off. But they bring a sumptuous atmosphere and sense of history to a garden, and I'm afraid I am smitten.

Some, like 'Céleste', with grey-green leaves and semi-double soft pink flowers, make rather good transition plants between the more natural and more formal areas of a garden, but those with fully double rosettes are definitely a fancy addition to a border. They look best in the civilized surroundings of hedges, topiary and gravel walks, as in the walled garden at Haseley Court, where they are grown, tightly packed, in narrow box-edged beds in a mist of catmint, spiked by pink and white foxgloves, with here and there the soft yellow glow of *Phlomis russeliana*, *Alchemilla mollis*, or the daylily *Hemerocallis* 'Golden Chimes'.

It is very hard to narrow the field when it comes to selecting old shrub roses, but here goes. I think the best of the dark wine-crimsons are 'Tuscany Superb' and 'William Lobb'. This last, the colour of fading velvet curtains, is quite a tall grower, and good leaning against a wall or up a pillar, as at Kiftsgate, where it is partnered with the rambler rose 'Bleu Magenta'. I rate 'Madame Hardy' the best white, 'Maiden's Blush' the best pale pink, and 'La Ville de Bruxelles' the best rich pink. Alba roses like 'Maiden's Blush' and 'Céleste' are, like the wilder shrub roses I have mentioned above, much less prone to mildew and blackspot problems: with the rest, you are often forced into fungicide spraying.

These shrub roses bloom only at midsummer, so where space is at a real premium and you want an old-world flavour, I would opt, first and foremost, for 'De Rescht', a short, compact rose which keeps on producing crimson cockades long after its main flush – terrific with greys and blues. 'Louise Odier' is quite a good deep pink counterpart.

The other option is to go for the Hybrid Musks. I think if I could only have two shrub roses in my garden, I would go for 'Buff Beauty' and pink 'Felicia'. Though they are more modern in appearance, they put on a spectacular show not only in early July but again in September. They are usually disease-free, and have a powerful airborne scent. Put next to a wall or tree, they will also ascend 10 feet or more.

As for sophisticated climbing roses, soft pink, healthy-leaved 'New Dawn' heads my list. You get one midsummer flush, and then sporadic blooms later. It is the same with apricot 'Climbing Lady Hillingdon' ('no good in bed but great up against a wall', as Helen Dillon says) and crimson-red 'Climbing Étoile de Hollande'. 'Mme Grégoire Staechelin' is a fine full-bodied pink but only blooms once. For shadier walls, I would go for 'Maigold', an early amber-yellow, or magenta-pink 'Zéphirine Drouhin' (though very prone to mildew). While to carry old-world exuberance up into the air, I would pick 'Félicité Perpétue', which has white flowers from pink buds, pink 'Blush Noisette', or 'Alister Stella Gray', which is amber and cream. These last two repeat-flower well. I can't

→ | The door at Haseley Court invites you into the intoxicating world of midsummer roses. But don't go mad at home: most shrub roses look dreadful for forty-six weeks of the year.

understand the popularity of 'Iceberg' – a cheerless, scentless, blackspot-prone waste of space.

PERENNIALS FOR PART-SHADY BORDER FRINGES

Where sunny border drifts into part shade, including under and around shrub roses, there are now plenty of meadow perennial candidates. At home, my old roses grow around a small circular lawn, fringed by apple trees and symmetrical pairs of dome-shaped box bushes (I did have vertical Irish junipers originally, but they looked attractively like lamp-posts to our two male Alsatians, and soon turned brown).

Here, the most valuable tribe of perennials are the hardy geraniums, or cranesbills. Deservedly popular, they include a number of foolproof species, delighted to grow wherever they are put, in sun or light shade. Some, like *G. sylvaticum* 'Album', pink-veined *G. clarkei* 'Kashmir White' and 'Kashmir Blue', and violet-blue 'Johnson's Blue', are handy for coming in May. They coincide with many of the wilder shrub roses but are usually going over by the time the more sophisticated roses get into their stride towards the end of June.

Black-eyed, magenta-pink *G. psilostemon* is essential for introducing a bit of

oomph among the pastels, beautiful next to grey and bluish leaves. 'Patricia' is a splendid plant of the same ilk, somewhat shorter, with a much longer flowering season. And for the rougher corners, where the borders disappear under the Portugal laurels, I use the more vigorous, ground-covering pinks of *G. endressii* and *G. × oxonianum* varieties. All these overlap in season with the old roses, as do the violet-blues of *G. pratense* and its long-flowering double cultivar 'Plenum Violaceum'.

The other perennial I consider indispensable is honey-scented *Viola cornuta*, in its purple, white, and lilac versions. The flowering stems of this mat-forming violet have the habit of filtering through their neighbours, knitting everything together in relaxed fashion.

For potent scent, I go for *Lilium regale*, but since it is not reliably perennial here, I grow several in a black pot (less obtrusive than orange) stood in the border, disguised by catmint foliage. This will be where a gap has appeared or I want an extra focal point. I will also slip in a pot of lilies on the terrace, as well as in the footrest behind the driver's seat – aromatherapy for long car journeys.

MEADOW BORDERS

My main sunny border, west-facing and on typically moist loamy soil, is geared towards summer, and divided into several early and late season sections. Come May, as the bulbs are fading, I get the first splashes of summer action. These are from two euphorbias, *E. griffithii* 'Dixter', with coppery leaves and burnt orange heads, and *E. palustris*, a 3ft/1m well-behaved clump-former in lime-green. I grow them in close proximity to complement each other – two colour versions of the same, or a similar, plant, often works well as a recipe – among the grassy leaves of late-flowering daylilies.

In June, the other end of the border turns yellow and violet, with *Phlomis russeliana* surrounded by two hardy geraniums, 'Johnson's Blue' and the slightly more purple *G. × magnificum*, and lilac *Viola cornuta*. I repeat these geraniums at intervals through the border, together with lime-green *Alchemilla*

← | *Lilium regale* is the supreme midsummer pot plant.

mollis; after flowering, all these can be shaved to the ground, and will come back with a fresh mound of leaves, so they keep on looking presentable.

I like the combination of geraniums and alchemilla, and suggested it as a theme in the Fellows' Garden at Lincoln College, Oxford. Anything I should know about the borders? I asked. 'We think there are two coffins in them somewhere,' came the reply. But I never encountered them.

As the phlomis reaches a climax, the daylily *Hemerocallis* 'Golden Chimes' begins to open its soft orange, maroon-backed trumpets behind. While a little further along, the earlier lemon *H. lilioasphodelus* (syn. *H. flava*) is at full tilt in front of another pool of 'Johnson's Blue'.

The later-flowering sections of border provide a green foil for these groups of early performers, among the principal assets being great sheaves of tall, sword-shaped crocosmia leaves, backed by drifts of plume poppy, *Macleaya cordata*, with huge blue, silver-backed foliage.

But if you think such leafy expanses of late perennials need jollying up earlier, the plants to use are the perennial poppies, *Papaver orientale*. They give a flamboyant shot of flower, with their huge black-botched saucers, and yet hardly take up any room, since they can be cut down after flowering. The orange and salmon colours (such as 'Mrs Perry') blend well together – if there is a yellow shrub rose in the background, like 'Frühlingsgold', so much the better. The salmons and pinks (like 'Karine') also work as a team, especially against silver leaves, such as a mound of jagged-leaved cardoon (*Cynara*). As for the whites (like 'Black and White'), the best partners I have seen are the red pincushion-flowered astrantias, such as 'Ruby Wedding'.

EARLY SUMMER SHADE

Once the tree and shrub leaves have expanded, the options for bringing colour into shady areas lessen. Hydrangeas, fuchsias and other shrubs will be on the scene shortly, but in the meantime there are a few notable perennial acts.

Given a spot of moisture in the soil, *Aruncus dioicus* is a deserving

← There is a host of indifferent astrantias masquerading as 'Shaggy' ('Margery Fish'), but the true plant (*top*) is a marvel, with long green-tipped bracts. *Geranium* 'Patricia' (*bottom*) is a valuable new introduction, flowering for many weeks.

candidate. Sprouting out of the fading bluebells and forget-me-nots, its huge, creamy, astilbe-like flower plumes open on 5ft/1.5m stems in June. Its cut leaves look good among hostas. A male form should be sought – the females have a shorter season and drop copious seed.

The pink and white forms of turk's-cap lily, *Lilium martagon*, can be naturalized in a grass glade – but don't make the mistake, as I once did, of

wandering dreamily through a colony, clothes brushing against them: you get yellow pollen stains in embarrassing places. They are equally at home in woodland borders, popping through the hellebore, fern and hosta leaves. Among the easiest lilies, they seem to take to acid and alkaline soils with equanimity.

Foxgloves give much the same effect in the shadows, and are now in full

bloom. I let them seed at will through my by now predominantly green winter border under the beech trees, and simply edit out those I don't want, or move them to better spots. In areas of the woodland garden at Knightshayes, they allow only the white form to colonize, which does make an ethereal picture.

At Kiftsgate, foxgloves give way on the sunnier woodland fringe to a favourite bellflower of mine, *Campanula latiloba* 'Highcliffe', an intense violet colour with large open flowers on stocky 2ft/60cm stems. It has a gently spreading habit, and I thought it merged beautifully there with self-seeding pale yellow *Sisyrinchium striatum* and pale pink *Linaria purpurea* 'Canon Went'.

For those with deep, cool, moist soil, neutral or acid, Himalayan blue poppies (*Meconopsis*) are worth a go. The one most commonly sold, *M. betonicifolia*, is seldom reliably perennial, and needs to be constantly renewed

from seed. Its hybrids with *M. grandis* are better in this respect: 'Slieve Donard' has fabulous turquoise tints. They really want a gritty soil, well laced with organic matter, which provides that seemingly paradoxical combination of summer moisture and excellent winter drainage. I try to provide it, but even so, these poppies remain slippery beasts, and I seldom seem to be able to stage much of a show.

On the other hand, with the giant Himalayan lily, *Cardiocrinum giganteum*, I have rendered visitors speechless. There are few more amazing sights in gardening: a lily bearing huge white, fragrant trumpets, flared crimson-red inside, on stems 8ft/2.5m high, solid as a rock. It is a plant that requires patience, for it takes three or four years to flower from a bought bulb. Then, the effort of flowering kills the parent bulb, leaving you offsets which require a similar length of time to mature. (To ensure continuity, I bought one fat bulb every year for four years.) All for a ten-day performance, invariably around Wimbledon week.

← Previous page: *Lilium martagon* will naturalize itself in thin grass in a moist, part-shaded spot, such as here at Haseley Court.

↑ The giant lily, *Cardiocrinum giganteum*, is the most arresting flowering plant hardy in the British Isles. There are many recipes for success; one Edwardian recommended a diet of salmon carcasses.

But the anticipation is worth it, getting even the postman and milkman on tenterhooks. In the off years, it produces lustrous heart-shaped leaves as good as a hosta (and equally appealing to slugs), and after flowering you get seedheads which swell like telegraph poles, eventually cracking open, drying brown, and lasting throughout the winter. It wants deep, fertile ground, somewhere bright but cool. There is a little forest of them along the stream at Wakehurst Place, Ardingly, Kew's outpost in Sussex, which I covet something rotten.

The Chilean flame flower, *Tropaeolum speciosum*, is another ooh-aah plant. In the cooler parts of the country, this herbaceous climber creates curtains of blood-scarlet up and across woodland shrubs yards long, but in the drier south it usually confines itself to the shady side of yew hedges (electrifying against golden yew at Dunham Massey, Cheshire). It wants moist ground, but the best advice is to plant several in different spots, and let it tell you where it likes.

SHADY WALLS

Out in June are the white lacecaps of the self-clinging climbing hydrangea, *H. anomala* subsp. *petiolaris*, one of the leading candidates for a shady wall – though slow to get started. It merges well with yellow-splashed ivies, and I have it tangled with the fruitily-scented, red-budded honeysuckle, *Lonicera* × *periclymenum* 'Serotina', on top of a low wall.

There are a number of honeysuckles that are happy in shade, including the scentless, apricot-orange *L.* × *tellmanniana* and the red *L. sempervirens*. The former looks good with the self-clinging vine, *Parthenocissus henryana*, whose bronze leaves take on bold white markings in shade; the latter is excellent with white rambler roses.

Some of the early, large-flowered clematis hybrids show up better in shade than in sun: among them, lavender-blue 'Lasurstern' and 'Mrs Cholmondeley', pure white 'Marie Boisselot' and white, green-striped 'Miss Bateman'. All these are in a different league to the dreaded mauve-pink 'Nelly Moser'.

OTHER EXCELLENT EARLY SUMMER-FLOWERING PLANTS

gravel and terrace	meadow borders	woodland glades
SHRUBS		
Buddleja alternifolia	◇ Potentilla fruticosa 'Primrose Beauty'	◆ Embothrium lanceolatum 'Ñorquinco'
◇ Deutzia setchuenensis var. corymbiflora	Potentilla fruticosa 'Vilmoriniana'	◇ Magnolia wilsonii
◆ Lupinus arboreus	◇ Rosa cultivars	
◇ Philadelphus microphyllus		
◆ Phlomis italica		
◆ Salvia lavandulifolia		
◇ Syringa pubescens var. microphylla 'Superba'		
SHRUBS & CLIMBERS *for sunny walls*		
◆ Carpenteria californica		◇ Lonicera caprifolium
◆ Fremontodendron californicum		◇ Lonicera tragophylla
Solanum crispum 'Glasnevin'		
BIENNIALS		
Oenothera stricta 'Sulfurea'		
Onopordon acanthium		
PERENNIALS		
Achillea 'Lucky Break'	Alstroemeria aurea (invasive)	Astrantia major
Anchusa azurea 'Loddon Royalist'	Baptisia australis	Astrantia major 'Shaggy'
Crambe cordifolia	Campanula latifolia var. alba	Campanula persicifolia cultivars
Dianthus carthusianorum	Cephalaria gigantea	Digitalis cultivars
Dianthus hybrids (pinks)	Clematis × durandii	Geranium phaeum 'Samobor'
Eremurus cultivars	Delphinium hybrids	Libertia formosa
Erodium cultivars	Geranium × magnificum	Paeonia mlokosewitschii
Euphorbia seguieriana subsp. niciciana	Lilium pyrenaicum	Paeonia obovata var. alba
Geranium cinereum cultivars	Morina longifolia	Polemonium caeruleum
	Persicaria bistorta 'Superba'	

gravel and terrace

PERENNIALS *cont.*

Geranium renardii
Geranium sanguineum
  cultivars
Helianthemum nummularium
  cultivars
Lilium candidum
Nectaroscordum siculum
  subsp. *bulgaricum*
Penstemon cultivars
Phlomis tuberosa 'Amazone'
Veronica spicata

meadow borders

Persicaria bistorta subsp.
  carnea
Persicaria polymorpha
Phuopsis stylosa
Potentilla atrosanguinea
Potentilla recta var.
  sulphurea
Symphytum caucasicum
  (invasive)
Thalictrum flavum glaucum

woodland glades

Saxifraga × urbium
Silene dioica cultivars
Silene fimbriata
Smilacina racemosa

GRASSES

Luzula nivea

FERNS

now with new fronds

Adiantum pedatum
Adiantum pedatum var.
  subpumilum
Adiantum venustum
Athyrium niponicum var.
  pictum
Dryopteris erythrosora
Dryopteris wallichiana
Polystichum setiferum
  Divisilobum Group

10 — LATE SUMMER

Around mid-July, another change starts to come over the garden as the early summer cast of shrubs and perennials dies away. The background freshness has gone, as the countryside matures to deep greens, browns and golds. Presenting this next wave of shrubs and perennials well means maintaining some sense of order and design amid the burgeoning growth. Serious sessions with shears and strimmer are *de rigueur*, and work wonders. I am like a gunfighter with my left-handed secateurs, whipping them out of their belt holster at the slightest provocation.

KEEPING GRAVEL AND MEDITERRANEAN BORDERS ALIGHT

Many of the low, hummocky Mediterranean shrubs are at their best in July. *Bupleurum fruticosum*, with bluish evergreen leaves and umbels of yellow flowers, makes a pleasant backdrop plant, good in tandem with the golden yellow of Spanish broom, *Spartium junceum*. Both bloom for months.

I have just been admiring this broom (together with marguerites, cistus and olearias) among the rock outcrops along the entrance drive into Portmeirion. This is Sir Clough Williams-Ellis's Italianate village on the north-west coast of Wales, built after 1925 to show how, using the best of architectural models, a new development can positively enhance a landscape, even one of staggering natural beauty: a lesson that was immediately lost on our town planners, needless to say.

← *Previous page:* Deep pink *Filipendula rubra* 'Venusta', and pale pink *F. palmata* 'Elegantissima', bloom through a sea of violet and white *Campanula lactiflora* at The Garden House.

→ *Right:* Ornamental grasses, including creamy *Stipa tenuissima*, rust-red *Carex buchananii*, and a fountain of *Stipa gigantea*, help to keep Lady Farm's steppe garden lively.

Lavender, planted in lines and patterns, is a traditional summer theme plant for terraces. John Brookes, our leading garden designer, calls this 'the old ladies' look' – all such rude remarks accompanied by an infectious machine-gun giggle – but I wouldn't be put off. It comes in various shades from deep purple ('Hidcote') and soft violet ('Munstead') to white ('Alba') and pink ('Loddon Pink'). The buttons of cotton lavender, *Santolina chamaecyparissus* (strong yellow) and *S. pinnata* subsp. *neapolitana* (creamy yellow), complement it perfectly, as you can see around the formal lily pool at Hidcote Manor, Gloucestershire, where yellow-edged agaves preside in pots.

The more naturalistic use of lavender, equally appealing, you meet in the German 'steppe' gardens, where it is grown in casual drifts, spiked by yellow *Verbascum olympicum* and the white stars of *Gaura lindheimeri*.

My favourite butterfly bush, *Buddleja* 'Lochinch', with deep blue-violet flowers and grey leaves, picks up the colour scheme splendidly. Perversely, here in North Wales the butterflies tend to arrive in quantity a couple of weeks after this and the other common buddleias have finished. So I also grow *B. davidii* 'Dartmoor', a variety with branched flowerheads in reddish-purple. It peaks in August, and indeed is then one of the showiest shrubs in the garden.

As for herbaceous focal points, the prime candidates are flowering yuccas

(such as *Y. recurvifolia*), the silver, jagged leaves of cardoon (*Cynara*), and the massive purple and white spires of acanthus, which last until the autumn. I am redoing my summer terrace border, and am about to plant all three (though

cardoon gets terrible blackfly here, and needs dousing in soapy water).

I think *Acanthus mollis* has the edge over *A. spinosus*, being less prickly, less prone to mildew, and with glossy leaves that persist well into the winter, given mild weather. In Oakland, California, Marcia Donahue has a run of it planted either side of the shady pathway beside the house (in the UK, acanthus grows but doesn't flower well in shade), an architectural and engagingly exotic treatment I thought, which leads to a garden gate made in the shape of a giant black hand. The sort of feature Indiana Jones might encounter.

At Lady Farm, Judy Pearce's steppe garden is by now speckled gold with clumps of daisy-flowered *Coreopsis verticillata*, growing among the low grasses and silvers of artemisias. Also out are the huge yellow saucers of the prostrate evening primrose, *Oenothera macrocarpa* (syn. *O. missouriensis*), and the metallic blue thistles of the sea holly *Eryngium bourgatii* – one of many good species, including the biennial *E. giganteum*, known as Miss Willmott's Ghost after that formidable Edwardian who employed eighty gardeners and was eventually bankrupted by her gardening mania – a warning to us all.

A TASTE OF SOUTH AFRICA

Since this is the holiday season, and the weather is often hot and humid, a touch of the exotic doesn't go amiss. The way to achieve it in the sunny terrace border is to mix in South African perennials.

↑ Spiky perennials, such as sea hollies (*Eryngium*), mix well with the summer daisy shapes.

At Killerton, near Exeter, the eyecatcher is the broad blue-leaved, orange-flowered poker *Kniphofia caulescens*, an exciting evergreen that is a lot hardier than it looks. It sits in front of a cloud of skeletal, lilac *Verbena bonariensis*, an association which I am about to pinch, putting in the foreground a drift of the low marjoram, *Origanum laevigatum* 'Herrenhausen', whose purplish flowers are at their best in August. (It also combines well with the pale blue hardy plumbago, *Ceratostigma willmottianum*.)

Hardy agapanthus are a prime source of mid-height flowers, planted in a medley of inky ('Bressingham Blue' and dwarf 'Tinkerbell'), sky-blue ('Ben Hope' and 'Isis'), and white ('Ardernei' and *A. campanulatus* var. *albidus*) shades, the mopheads presented on tall stems above lush, straplike leaves. Invariably, the hardy *Salvia* × *sylvestris* 'Mainacht' is producing a second crop of deep violet spikes at the same time, and I like to weave that among them. The scented double white soapwort, *Saponaria officinalis* 'Alba Plena', I also introduced on the recommendation of the garden writer Robin Lane Fox, to complete the trio. A beautiful thing and not particularly invasive.

At Killerton, *Agapanthus* 'Ben Hope' is grown in front of the tall, silver-leaved *Perovskia atriplicifolia* – the haze of violet-blue, catmint-like flowers a terrific contrast to the solid globes of the agapanthus. With its long flowering season, perovskia is a perennial to take seriously.

The same goes for *Aster* × *frikartii* 'Mönch' (or 'Wunder von Stäfa' – no one seems to know the difference). In bloom for months, this 3ft/1m lavender-blue daisy is well worth repeating along a border, and looks terrific between the flat heads of *Sedum* 'Herbstfreude' and the silver leaves of *Artemisia* 'Powis Castle'; it usually needs staking. *A. thomsonii* 'Nanus', its dwarf counterpart for the front of the border, has an equally long season.

For colour contrast, the summer-flowering poker hybrids are just the ticket. Among the most dependable are 'Sunningdale Yellow', orange-red 'Samuel's Sensation', coral and cream 'Jenny Bloom', and caramel and cream 'Toffee Nosed'; creamy 'Little Maid' and orange 'Bressingham Comet' are good short ones.

Areas composed entirely of plants with grassy and straplike leaves can be very appealing. I don't mean borders exclusively of ornamental grasses, which are a bore, but borders where there is a range of flower shapes and colours. I suppose it is because it looks like an exotic meadow. The poet James Fenton has an effective formal one in his Oxford garden. He first came into my consciousness as an unlikely explorer in Redmond O'Hanlon's travelogue *Into the Heart of Borneo*, reading Victor Hugo as their dugout canoe navigated rapids in deepest rainforest. And his survival was a particular comfort to me because at the time I was planning a very similar journey into Papua New Guinea.

This sort of grassy-leaved border can be structured by hefty yuccas and can comprise pokers, agapanthus, miscanthus and pampas grasses, and bulbs of the

↑ *Dierama pulcherrimum* arches over a grass path at The Garden House.

Cape hyacinth, *Galtonia candicans*, which is also sporting its candelabra of white bells now. A mass of bulbs in spring can give a second season.

Don't overlook *Tulbaghia violacea*, another short bulbous Cape plant, with grassy leaves and agapanthus-like heads in lilac. The marvel is that it blooms in at least two flushes, the last one combining well with the stars of short mountain asters (*Aster amellus*) like 'Veilchenkoenigin'. Earlier on, it is attractive among the pink-shaded, blue foliage of *Sedum telephium* subsp. *ruprechtii* – one of the very best of the sedum tribe.

For terrace paving cracks, the South African Venus's fishing-rod, *Dierama pulcherrimum*, is the leading candidate. The dangling pink bells, borne on tall arching stems above grassy leaves, seed freely in the borders at The Garden House, but in most gardens it is more reliable where it can get its roots under stone and paving slabs, cool and protected. There are many rare colour forms of it, and of its shorter relative, *D. dracomontanum* (syn. *D. pumilum*). The white herbaceous mallow, *Malva moschata* f. *alba*, is more foolproof, and another top-notch paving-crack perennial.

SUNNY WALLS

August is not a month that looks after itself. In fact, after November and December I rate it as the most testing period. So it is always worth doing a spot of garden visiting to see how others keep the show on the road. Powis Castle doesn't disappoint. One of the most sensational plants on the terrace walls at this time is the Cape figwort, *Phygelius capensis*. Usually seen as a border perennial, against a wall it transforms itself into a shrub, producing a shower of scarlet funnels, 8ft/2.5m high, for months on end.

Further along the same wall you meet *Itea ilicifolia*, an evergreen, holly-like shrub which is now a waterfall of lime-green, honey-scented flowers resembling the sprays of millet you put in the budgie's cage. I have it at home with red fuchsia and the annual climber *Eccremocarpus scaber* scrambling through it. I say annual, but this orange-funnelled twiner often survives for several years,

and when it eventually succumbs it obligingly leaves you copious quantities of seed with which to start again. It is a valuable plant for clothing the bare stems of climbing roses.

This role is also perfectly suited to the starry-flowered Viticella clematis, which bloom from midsummer onwards in sun and part shade, up trees and pergolas, walls and shrubs, and give new life to many a garden backdrop. They are usually extremely vigorous (so need hard pruning in early spring), and don't get wilt disease. Green-tipped, white 'Alba Luxurians', crimson-red 'Madame Julia Correvon', purple and white 'Minuet', velvet-red 'Kermesina', purple-black 'Black Prince' and the extraordinary double plum-purple 'Purpurea Elegans Plena' are among the best.

TENDER PERENNIALS IN POTS

One of the longest-lasting sources of summer colour, from the beginning of June to the frost, comes from tender perennials. The beefier and taller sorts, like dahlias, cannas and 5ft/1.5m salvias, are destined for the border, but the others are made for pots.

Esther Merton's approach at The Old Rectory, Burghfield, was to assemble a line of enormous terracotta cauldrons along her terrace, stuffed with so many different plants that by July there were some serious explosions.

In one of the most memorable, she had a yellow-edged agave as an architectural eyecatcher, a green-leaved *Hosta plantaginea*, and gold, starry-flowered *Bidens ferulifolia* and lemon-leaved *Helichrysum petiolare* 'Limelight' spilling down the sides; for mid-height, the soft yellow daisies of *Argyranthemum* 'Jamaica Primrose', merged for contrast with blue *Verbena* 'Loveliness' (scrumptious suntan-lotion scent); and as the tallest ingredients, the purple saucers of *Tibouchina semidecandra*, the lime-green foliage of a young *Euphorbia mellifera*, the primrose bells of *Abutilon* 'Canary Bird', and a

↑ *Clematis* 'Black Prince' is worth hunting down.
→ When the tulips are over, I bring out pelargoniums like 'The Boar' (*left*) and half-hardy exotics like *Agave americana* 'Variegata' (*right*) to contrast with the pots of blue-leaved *Echeveria secunda* var. *glauca*. Blue and white *Agapanthus africanus* carry the torch into August.

shower of apricot turk's-cap lilies. But the watering and feeding programme is not for the faint-hearted. And you can forget going away on holiday.

Her pots were planted *in situ*, when danger of serious frost had passed (around the end of May), and when they were dismantled in the autumn, certain plants would be potted up for use next year and overwintered under glass. Cuttings would be taken of others. This is a palaver. Back home, I wouldn't feel in the least guilty about throwing or giving everything away, exactly as you would with annual bedding. After all, the nurseries do a much better job of producing appetizing young plants for next year than the time-pressured amateur. What's more, you may well fancy growing something different.

An alternative, more manageable, approach to container gardening is to have an assembly of smaller pots, with just one sort of plant growing in each. This is what I do, around the cones of box on my terrace. You don't need a sacktruck or team of weightlifters to carry them about, you can rearrange them as you like, and at the end of the season any permanent ingredients can be taken indoors intact. Many will also not be so demanding on water. Indeed, one summer a mouse managed to raise a nest of young in one of my pots of pelargoniums; it was only when I noticed a strange lump in the soil, and pressed down hard, that the family erupted out, like a scene from *Alien*.

My display kicks off in May with tulips and a few companion plants. Last year it was black tulips, scented white rhododendrons, and the blue rosettes of the succulent *Echeveria secunda* var. *glauca*, bearing orange, urn-shaped

flowers. Very sophisticated. Bronze and yellow-striped phormiums stand about right through the season as bold contrast plants.

From June onwards, the company will certainly include a fuchsia like 'Thalia', with pencil-slim funnels of scarlet over purplish leaves (sometimes with trailing sky-blue lobelia, or violet Swan River daisy, *Brachyscome iberidifolia*); perhaps a scented purple heliotrope or orange *Mimulus aurantiacus*; and various pelargoniums – my favourites being damson 'Lord Bute', and the semi-prostrate salmon 'The Boar' and crimson-red 'Mrs Kingsley'.

By August there will be balls of blue and white flower above the evergreen leaves of tender *Agapanthus africanus*. Plants are expensive to buy, and need housing in a frost-free greenhouse or porch for the winter, but they are well worth it, fattening into buxom clumps (so much so that they often burst clay pots; black plastic ones are safer), and flowering for weeks on end.

For shade, I think the best options for pots are traditional bell-shaped fuchsias, busy lizzies (there are some handsome double forms, in salmon and white) and red-funnelled *Cestrum* 'Newellii', as well as hostas and hydrangeas.

I follow Mrs Merton's former gardener, Susan Dickenson, in using a predominantly John Innes No. 2 loam-based potting compost, lightened with a bit of perlite and peat-substitute. This anchors the pots properly against the wind, and is easy to re-wet when dry.

HOT COLOURS FOR MEADOW BORDERS

July in the walled garden borders at The Garden House belongs to *Campanula lactiflora*, which creates clouds of violet-blue bells (deep violet in 'Prichard's Variety', white in 'Alba'). It is one of the best backdrop plants of the season. Here, it sets off the fluffy rose-pink plumes of the tall prairie meadowsweet, *Filipendula rubra* 'Venusta'.

Even better, further along the grass path, it is the foil for a medley of yellow, red and orange daylilies. I have admired this combination in Germany, too.

Many of the later daylilies go on flowering for many weeks, given sunlight and a little moisture in the soil, but to keep up the display, they may need dividing every few years.

Having attracted the attention of breeders, especially in America, there are now thousands of daylily varieties, including many horrors. Favourites of mine are lemon 'Hyperion' and 'Marion Vaughn', soft orange 'Burning Daylight' and 'Mauna Loa', lemon-white 'Joan Senior', and deep red 'Stafford' and 'Oriental Ruby'. But you should pay a visit to Diana Grenfell's collection at Apple Court Nursery, Hordle, in the New Forest, to see the options. She grows them with pokers, blue agapanthus, and the elegant grass *Deschampsia cespitosa*, which produces feathery plumes of bronze and gold in summer.

Heavily influenced by Powis Castle, my own main border turns to hot colours in August with the orange flagon-shaped hips of the rose 'Geranium', a compact upright shrub which bears single red flowers in June, like stamps of sealing-wax. The arching yellow-striped leaves of the tall grass *Miscanthus sinensis* 'Zebrinus' grow behind it, and below, across the green ridge of tree peony and skimmia leaves, are sheaves of crocosmias – relatives of the invasive common orange montbretia.

Like many South African perennials, crocosmias like a soil that is well-drained but has some body to it; they were hopeless in my dry, silty Oxford soil, the leaves searing and becoming martyrs to red spider mite. The tall scarlet 'Lucifer' is the best known of the taller ones, but it performs in July (at the same time as that other striking scarlet, the Maltese cross, *Lychnis chalcedonica*, and white Shasta daisies, *Leucanthemum × superbum* varieties; it also looks good in front of *Campanula lactiflora*).

For August, I go for the similar 'Emberglow', and orange *C. paniculata*. Of the shorter varieties, which do much better in the cooler, moister counties, I like apricot-yellow 'Citronella' and 'Solfatare', the latter with bronze leaves; they benefit from being divided every few years. Blue-leaved *Macleaya cordata* or *M. microcarpa* 'Kelway's Coral Plume', now in flower, is the backdrop plant used at Powis for the taller crocosmias, and I can't better it. White Japanese anemones work well behind the shorter ones.

A WILDER BORDER LOOK

Phloxes can be a mainstay of the high summer border. A few years ago Fergus Garrett, head gardener at Great Dixter, introduced me to small-flowered, lilac-pink *Phlox paniculata*, the parent of all the hybrids. It overlaps in season with *Campanula lactiflora*, and at Bodnant, North Wales, the two are repeated along a border, combined with the cream plumes of *Artemisia lactiflora* (best in its purplish-leaved variant Guizhou Group). *P. paniculata* 'Alba Grandiflora' and 'Fujiyama' are good small-flowered whites.

Phlox hybrids are potently Edwardian used *en masse*, but in his garden at Ruinen, Ton ter Linden brought them into the modern idiom by having them in bands, broken by very simple plants like self-seeding annual teasel and purple-leaved orach (*Atriplex hortensis* var. *rubra*), and the untidy mopheads of purple bergamots (*Monarda fistulosa* hybrids).

The plants in his borders were all much the same height, as in a meadow. The play was in the densities: a solid block of one flower seen through a

transparent veil of a flimsier flower. And here and there would be a dramatic eruption of some luminous tall perennial, like the white waterfall of *Sanguisorba tenuifolia* 'Alba', or the lilac starburst of *Thalictrum delavayi*.

I thought the best part was the yellow borders, either side of a winding grass path. Here, the filigree shapes of *Solidago* 'Goldenmosa' and silver *Artemisia ludoviciana* (invasive) were repeated as a matrix, and through it grew yellow and rusty-orange daisy-flowered heleniums and trumpet-flowered daylilies. In clumps behind was the best tall daisy of late summer, soft lemon *Helianthus* 'Lemon Queen'. But the making of the scene was the fact that the entire company was set in a forest of self-sown purple orach seedlings, which by late summer were flopping over everything with theatrical campness.

The key to an atmospheric garden is that sense, whether true or not, that nature has just about got the upper hand (or, as Robin Lane Fox puts it, that the owner has died three weeks previously). You certainly felt that here.

PONDSIDE PLANTING

By now, my own pond tends to look like an alligator swamp, and it is time for an afternoon's blanket-weed extraction with the rake, and duckweed skimming with the telescopic-handled fishing net to reveal the water.

The white water hawthorn (*Aponogeton distachyos*) and water irises (purple *I. laevigata*, yellow *I. pseudacorus* and its creamy version 'Bastardii') are over. But there are still waterlilies – my favourite being 'Marliacea Chromatella', with sulphur flowers and purple-splashed leaves; it looks good with goldfish and golden orfe (I say wistfully; the heron has polished them off again). Cyperus sedges are in bloom, and there are fat violet-blue cones above the arrowhead leaves of pickerel weed, *Pontederia cordata*. I don't like the pond too jazzy, so I have avoided florist's arum, *Zantedeschia aethiopica*, but in another setting the tropical impact of its large white spathes and canna-like leaves would be splendid.

Late summer in Lorna MacMahon's stream garden within her Galway hazel

← | *Helianthus* 'Lemon Queen' produces a terrific crop of daisies on 6ft/2m stems, but needs staking.

wood is marked by a flush of yellow bells from the giant Himalayan cowslip, *Primula florindae*. It freely colonizes damp soil, and has a lemon scent that carries for yards. In one spot, they swirl around a massive yellow-edged phormium. In the wild in New Zealand, I have seen *Phormium tenax* growing in bogs (*P. cookianum* grows on cliffs), but, as in Galway, the water is not subjected to prolonged freezing; in colder climates, it is safer to give phormiums decent drainage.

For colour contrast, she uses the lilac of blue-leaved hostas, now in flower, and the spikes of purple loosestrife, *Lythrum salicaria*. There are some excellent forms of this, including rose-pink 'Feuerkerze' and pale pink 'Blush'. The orange daisies of purple-leaved *Ligularia dentata* 'Desdemona' (combined with creamy meadowsweet, *Filipendula ulmaria*, in my garden), and red spires of lobelias add further sparks.

Further along, there is a glade of feathery astilbes in reds, pinks and whites, merged with hostas. These plants don't do much for me, with one exception. That is the tongue-twister *A. chinensis* var. *taquetii* 'Purpurlanze', with magenta plumes; it doesn't need very moist ground.

In Ensköping, Sweden, Piet Oudolf combines it with the tall purplish-grey grass *Molinia caerulea* subsp. *arundinacea* 'Transparent', with the wine-coloured globes of *Angelica gigas* and the dark cones of teasel nearby. The shadows cast on the paths by all these sculptural plants were mesmerizing. Somewhere else I saw an arresting pairing between this astilbe and the lime-green of the excellent summer-flowering euphorbia *E. schillingii*.

WOODLAND GLADES AND SHADY WALLS

Hydrangeas are the principal summer-flowering shrubs for shady borders, thriving where conditions are not too dark or dry. My own favourites are the larger species, with lilac lacecaps and velvet leaves. *H. aspera* Villosa Group in particular is a real star, at its best in August; at Chirk Castle near Wrexham it

→ *Gillenia trifoliata* is an airy perennial for light shade, with flowerheads that remain attractive after the petals have dropped.

sits below a shady wall which is covered in the lilac-blue clematis 'Perle d'Azur', one of the finest of the late hybrids. *H. aspera* subsp. *sargentiana*, with larger, tropically sized foliage and pale flowerheads, stands beside the door of Nick and Pam Coote's Oxford house behind big blue-leaved hostas.

At Dunham Massey, near Altrincham, I noticed how well the shorter lacecap and mophead varieties contrasted with grasses. I think it was *H. arborescens* 'Annabelle' I saw there – anyway, with its balls of small, creamy white blossom, it is the pick of the pack. And it was growing with the slim *Miscanthus sinensis* 'Gracillimus'. This could be developed into a repeating theme, perhaps incorporating the lacecap 'Lanarth White', the white mophead 'Mme Émile Mouillère', and feathery *Deschampsia* grasses.

Other white-flowered shrubs that really stand out against the heavy shade are the acid-loving eucryphias. Smothered in white cups in August, *E.* × *nymansensis* 'Nymansay' makes a tall evergreen column, *E. glutinosa* a more rounded, deciduous bush. Both are terrific with blue hydrangeas.

Otherwise, I think the best partners for these woodland whites are scarlet, purple-skirted fuchsias, either the ordinary, small-flowered *F.* 'Riccartonii' or the more glamorous 'Mrs Popple'. Both are hardy, though 'Mrs Popple' gets its top growth killed in cold winters. Given a wall behind, a rich purple large-flowered clematis like 'Jackmanii' would be good behind 'Riccartonii'. As with sunny walls, there are a great many clematis options now; pale blue-violet 'Prince Charles' and reddish-purple 'Venosa Violacea' make a showy pairing on a part-shady wall at Lady Farm.

There are also a few good perennials to rise up out of the tapestry of ferns, hostas and other ground-dwellers. Around midsummer, *Gillenia trifoliata* gives a burst of white stars from flame-coloured flower stalks, and then I look to *Persicaria campanulata*, which produces panicles of tiny bells non-stop from July until

the autumn. It comes in shades of rose, pale pink and white; a mixture is an improvement on a single colour.

In another spot, where sunny meadow border drifts into shade, I have a trio of perennials: tall purple monkshood, *Aconitum* 'Spark's Variety', shaggy red mophead bergamot, *Monarda didyma* 'Cambridge Scarlet', and the yellow daisy *Inula hookeri* (mildly invasive). You don't expect strong colour in a shady late summer garden.

OTHER EXCELLENT LATE SUMMER-FLOWERING PLANTS

gravel and terrace	meadow borders	woodland glades
SHRUBS		
Abelia × grandiflora		Clerodendrum bungei
Ceanothus × delileanus		Hohena lyallii
'Gloire de Versailles'		Leycesteria formosa
Cotinus coggygria		Rhododendron
Escallonia 'Iveyi'		auriculatum
Escallonia rubra 'Crimson		Rhododendron decorum
Spire'		Sorbaria tomentosa var.
Hebe 'Great Orme'		angustifolia
Hyssopus officinalis		
Indigofera heterantha		
Jasminum humile		
'Revolutum'		
Lavatera 'Barnsley'		
Lavatera 'Kew Rose'		
Lotus hirsutus		

SHRUBS & CLIMBERS

for sunny walls		for shady walls
Buddleja crispa		Jasminum officinale
Buddleja × weyeriana		Pileostegia viburnoides
'Golden Glow'		Schizophragma
Salvia microphylla		integrifolium

gravel and terrace

SHRUBS & CLIMBERS

for sunny walls (cont.)

- Trachelospermum
    asiaticum
- Trachelospermum
    jasminoides

PERENNIALS

Achillea 'Lachskönigin'

Alcea hybrids

Alcea rugosa

Alstroemeria hybrids

Anaphalis triplinervis

Calamintha nepeta

Filipendula vulgaris
  'Multiplex'

Gaura lindheimeri 'Siskyou
  Pink'

Geranium × riversleaianum
  'Russell Prichard'

Geranium wallichianum
  'Buxton's Variety'

Gypsophila paniculata
  'Bristol Fairy'

Gypsophila 'Rosenschleier'

Limonium latifolium

Linum narbonense

Lobelia tupa

Platycodon grandiflorus

Romneya coulteri

Scabiosa graminifolia

Verbena rigida

meadow borders

Achillea ageratum 'W. B.
  Child'

Delphinium 'Alice Artindale'

Delphinium hybrids

Epilobium angustifolium var.
  album

Galega officinalis 'Alba'

Inula hookeri

Liatris spicata

Lilium 'Enchantment'

Lilium henryi

Lysimachia clethroides

Lysimachia ephemerum

Persicaria amplexicaulis
  'Firetail'

Verbena hastata cultivars

woodland glades

Actaea rubra

Anemone hupehensis
  cultivars

Anemone × hybrida cultivars

Lilium 'Black Beauty'

Lilium pardalinum

Lysimachia ciliata

Sinacalia tangutica

11 — AUTUMN

Total harmony descends on the garden as the foliage starts turning and falling, and there is that moist earthy smell in the air, enlivened by honeyed chrysanthemums. Kicking through the leaves, I am in no hurry to clear up: this is an untidy season, let's enjoy it. The borders are then selectively cut down, letting anything with good stems and seedheads stand until the spring.

THE EXOTIC GARDEN

The enthusiasm for High Victorian exotica has been rekindled, largely thanks to Christopher Lloyd ripping up his parents' rose garden at Great Dixter, Sussex ('the tearing roots music to my ears,' he wrote) and turning it into a jungle of lush foliage and flamboyant flowers – the impact all the more dramatic because the climax comes in late summer and early autumn, when many gardens are looking as if they have shot their bolt.

On such a scale, this involves a major annual operation which most of us can only goggle at. All those different paddle-leaved cannas, including yellow-striped 'Striata' and pink-striped 'Durban', and dahlias, like red 'Witteman's Superba' and purple 'Hillcrest Royal', need their fleshy roots storing, in slightly moist compost, in a frost-free cellar or outhouse. I met one cottage gardener who kept his dahlias, upside down in racks, behind his armchair in the sitting-room all winter; coal was the only source of heat, so around 6ft/2m from the fire was ideal for them.

Previous page: The prairie slope at Lady Farm reaches its climax in autumn. There is a dramatic colour change when the orange heleniums give way to swathes of yellow rudbeckias. The background haze is from the grass *Deschampsia cespitosa* 'Goldtau'.

Left: *Dahlia* 'Arabian Night' opens almost black and matures to blood red. It will stay black if picked.

Dixter's other exotica like begonias are lifted, repotted and taken under glass. And even the hardy trees in the rose garden are chopped back to a stump at the end of the winter to persuade them to produce a few huge leaves (like umbrella-leaved *Paulownia tomentosa*) or a crop of fresh juvenile leaves (like blue-leaved *Eucalyptus gunnii*); they will accept this for a number of years, before deciding 'sod this' and giving up the ghost.

Here at home, I can cope with just one tropical splash. I am currently playing a variation on the Lloyd theme with the superb orange, purple-leaved dahlia 'David Howard' and similar tinted canna 'Wyoming', set against the jagged blue leaves of *Melianthus major* (which can be left outside all year) and all in a haze of lilac *Verbena bonariensis*. The black-red dahlia 'Arabian Night' blends well with the pink domes of *Clerodendrum bungei*.

Along the terrace at Cottesbrooke Hall, Northamptonshire, where the narrow borders are punctuated by repeated outcrops of yuccas, the gardeners are experimenting with fleshy-rooted exotics left outside under mulches. This is not a warm part of Britain. But among the successes are the hooded, royal-blue-flowered *Salvia patens* (like ceratostigma, a magnet for hummingbird hawkmoths when they are about), well placed against blue-leaved hostas; red-black, chocolate-scented *Cosmos atrosanguineus*, growing among the tender daisies *Argyranthemum* 'Jamaica Primrose' and golden *Bidens ferulifolia*; and lilac *Dahlia merckii*, standing in a colony of *Verbena bonariensis*.

Occasionally I am in New York City in October, and at the first opportunity head for the Conservatory Garden in Central Park, an oasis on the borders of Harlem designed by Lynden Miller. Ten years ago, when Central Park was notorious, few New Yorkers dared venture there. (I like the story of the tourist who asked a policeman if he could get to a certain store by crossing the park. 'Sure,' replied the cop. 'But no one's ever made it.') But now that Manhattan is more civilized than Central London, the garden fills with strollers and picnickers.

The autumn borders are the best showcase for Mexican salvias I know. These are irresistible plants (alive with bees, hummingbirds and praying mantis in New York), but mostly thoroughly tender, so that you must either take cuttings from year to year, or buy afresh (the option I recommend, because you start with bushy plants which come into bloom sooner).

Of the many electrifying tall blues to be had, I like royal-blue *S. guaranitica* 'Blue Enigma' and 'Black and Blue', and *S. uliginosa*, a kingfisher azure, which combines well with *Verbena bonariensis*. It sometimes comes through the winter, as does *S. involucrata* 'Boutin', with pouched flowers in shocking pink – good with pale pink *Abelia grandiflora*, a stalwart background shrub of the season. *S. splendens* 'Van-Houttei' is a sumptuous cardinal red.

Another plant I find I have to purchase annually is *Gladiolus callianthus* 'Murielae'. Even when stored in a frost-free greenhouse, the bulbs are reluctant to bloom a second time. So I grow them in a pot on the terrace and discard them afterwards. The white, maroon-splashed stars, borne above tall leaves, are exceptionally elegant, but the principal point of them is the piercing sweet scent, which floats far on the evening air.

DRY GARDEN AND TERRACE

If it can get its roots into the cool moist soil under the paving cracks, *Persicaria vacciniifolia* is a ground-hugging perennial that really earns its keep, producing its wiry, pale pink spikes all through the late summer and autumn months. I have it along the top of a retaining wall, alternating with *Geranium sanguineum* and blue-leaved *Euphorbia characias*, and it hangs down in swags.

↑ Intense blue perennials are a rare commodity, so *Salvia uliginosa* is worth a little trouble. I dig up some roots and bring them indoors for the winter.

P. affinis 'Superba', with fatter pink and crimson flowers, makes more substantial ground-cover for sun and part shade, and is another principal provider of late colour.

Reliable old *Sedum* 'Herbstfreude' ('Autumn Joy'), you just can't do without it. There is no better lynchpin perennial for a sunny, well-drained border, respectable from the moment its fleshy leaves appear in spring to the moment its dried winter flowerheads are removed almost a year later. In August they are smothered in butterflies, and now they are maturing to deep red, a chunky contrast to the late-flushing catmint and the blue-violet of the short grey-leaved shrub *Caryopteris* × *clandonensis* 'Heavenly Blue'. A deep pink perennial, like ground-hugging *Diascia barberae* 'Ruby Field' or a plume of *Gaura lindheimeri* 'Siskiyou Pink', looks good in the mix.

In the Westpark in Munich, one of the best showcases of the naturalistic 'steppe' garden style, *Sedum* 'Herbstfreude' is used in short, informal ridges between drifts of mountain asters, *A. amellus*, such as the outstanding purple 'Veilchenkoenigin' ('Violet Queen'). Mounds of silver sage and lavender leaves give illumination, and behind are the tinting leaves and parchment flowerheads of grasses like *Stipa calamagrostis*.

I am a fan of the small-flowered asters such as lavender-violet *A. sedifolius* and its short form 'Nanus', and the maroon-bossed white *A. lateriflorus*

'Horizontalis', which produces its flowers in tiers in October – the black-green leaves are a punctuation point all summer (even darker in 'Prince'). All these are splendid with *Sedum* 'Herbstfreude', as indeed are lavender-blue *A.* × *frikartii* 'Mönch' and short *A. thomsonii* 'Nanus', which have been in bloom since August.

Further along the Westpark border I came upon a cloud of white *Gaura lindheimeri* silhouetting a stand of the late orange poker *Kniphofia triangularis* (syn. *K. galpinii*). That provided some nice crackle. Given shelter and very good drainage, you could also get a burst of scarlet from *Zauschneria californica* – handsome against sky-blue *Ceratostigma willmottianum*.

Two autumn-flowering bulbs that clump up readily are blue-violet *Crocus speciosus* – which, at the Westpark, is planted in tandem with silvery achillea leaves – and *Nerine bowdenii*, whose intense pink trumpets are carried on top of tall stems, naked of leaves. Unlike the crocus, which likes a bit of moisture in the ground and is happy even in part shade, nerines want to be roasted. The base of a south wall is traditionally recommended, in between the Algerian iris clumps, but as long as they get drainage and full exposure, this is not essential. They stand out well among silver shrubs, blue ceratostigma and the spent heads of agapanthus.

SUNNY WALLS

The gardens of Sutton Place, near Guildford, were designed by the celebrated landscape architect Sir Geoffrey Jellicoe, who died recently in his nineties. Like many landscape architects, he wasn't in the least interested in plants (in fact, I was told that in one university course the plant knowledge section was optional, and the budding landscape architects could opt for French instead; which explains many a deadly public shrubbery). So his planting plans were done by his wife, Susan.

There are several very attractive schemes here, one of which makes a late summer play of lavender, acanthus, purple sage, violet-blue *Veronica spicata*, and white-belled *Galtonia candicans*. And a little along the mellow Tudor brick walls, the tints are picked up by a buddleia, *Buddleja crispa*. With soft grey leaves and short cones of sweet-scented lilac flowers, this is a very different creature to the familiar butterfly bushes, and, in bloom from late summer onwards, is one of the most deserving wall shrubs.

So is its cousin *B. auriculata*. Dowdier, with darker grey leaves and creamy flowers, it scores in the fact that it has a delicious lemon-peel perfume and comes into bloom very late, peaking in November and still with a few flowers into the

← *Crocus speciosus* is an autumn highlight, though, like all crocuses, it is a martyr to wind and rain.

New Year. It is always on the Christmas dinner-table here. The books raise a query over its hardiness, but in my garden it lost no time racing to the eaves, and requires hard pruning every spring; *B. crispa* is a more modest shrub.

MEADOW BORDERS

The 'prairie garden' at Lady Farm gives colour from late summer until the frosts. Of course, it is simply a stylized evocation of real prairie, using mostly, but not exclusively, North American perennials.

Real prairie, or at least what remains of it (most of it has gone the way of the bison), is mingled as a meadow. And what really amazed me about it, looking at reconstructed morsels of tallgrass prairie (there is also shortgrass prairie) in Indiana, was its height. Before horses, the Great Plains Indians would have had to stand on each other's shoulders to avoid getting lost. It is an ecosystem regenerated by fire, and this keeps out colonizing woody plants. If you are sowing seeds of prairie plants at home, you often need intense heat (such as boiling water) to break dormancy.

A principal player on Lady Farm's moist, sunny slope is the coppery-red daisy *Helenium* 'Moerheim Beauty', set out in bands between the erect grass *Calamagrostis* × *acutiflora* 'Karl Foerster'. This outstanding perennial blooms in July and again in late August, if deadheaded. There are numerous other mid-height colour variants, like orange-yellow 'Wyndley', as well as taller ones, like mahogany-red 'Bruno' and yellow 'Butterpat', that bloom into September. The purplish-pink, orange-coned daisies of *Echinacea purpurea*, and its white cultivar 'White Swan', make arresting contrast.

As 'Moerheim Beauty' fades, it passes the torch to the yellow black-eyed Susans, *Rudbeckia fulgida* var. *deamii* and the slightly shorter *R. f.* var. *sullivantii* 'Goldsturm'. Big clumps of the tall purple Joe Pye weed, *Eupatorium purpureum* 'Atropurpureum', are by now in bloom to complement them. For many years Americans thought it hilarious that we grew this weed in our gardens, but now I see it appearing in theirs. The eco-movement is doing much

to alert gardeners to the fact that other countries' flowers are not always more beautiful than one's own. A fine plant, it grows well in part-shade as well as sun.

There are also plenty of feathery pink and silver plumes on the *Miscanthus*, the gardener's biggest tribe of ornamental grasses. The sheer number of almost identical, mostly German, selections is baffling, not least to me, but luckily Roger Grounds has made a study of them in his garden at Apple Court, Hampshire. He rates 'Malepartus', 'Rotsilber', and 'Flamingo' among the best early-flowering 5ft/1.5m ones (opening red-brown in July, and maturing to silky white); and of those that start a little later, 6ft/2m 'Graziella',

↑ | Purple coneflower, *Echinacea purpurea*, is a moisture-loving prairie plant of dazzling beauty; it can be short-lived.

4ft/1.25m 'Undine', and 3ft/1m 'Kleine Silberspinne'. Most of these feature at Lady Farm.

The biggest tribe of autumn daisies are the asters. In America you see them popping out of rough grass on the edges of woods, and in the garden the blue-violet forms in particular look very much at home among those ornamental prairie grasses that take on fiery red and yellow tints, like *Andropogon gerardii* and *Panicum virgatum* 'Rehbraun' or 'Hänse Herms'. I think the best lavender-blue asters for this company are 4ft/1.25m *A. turbinellus*, 5ft/1.5m 'Little Carlow', and 6ft/2m *A. cordifolius* 'Chieftain'.

For a proper Edwardian aster splash, I would go for the fresh green New England hybrids (*A. novae-angliae*) over and above the New York hybrids (*A. novae-belgii*), which have miserable dark foliage, invariably adorned with mildew. Soft 'Harrington's Pink', rose-pink 'Rosa Sieger' and shocking cerise 'Andenken an Alma Pötschke' make a fine team. As white companions for these, and the blue asters above, I would pick 3ft/1m *A. pringlei* 'Monte Cassino' and 5ft/1.5m *A. cordifolius* 'Elegans'.

Highlights of my own main border in October are the hardy perennial chrysanthemums. With flowers the size of buttons and neat, self-supporting domes of small leaves, they look presentable all summer. Rose-pink 'Anastasia' is a great contrast to the autumnal silvers and blues; 'Bronze Elegance' is perfect for picking up the orange tints of shrub rose hips – a particularly generous crop is produced by *R. moyesii* and our native hedgerow rose *R. eglanteria*, with apple-scented leaves.

Netta Statham reckoned that the September-flowering bulbous colchicums, or naked ladies, were the perfect plants to put between clumps of midsummer hardy geraniums. The one takes over from the other, and if you shave your geraniums back in summer, you have a fresh foil for the huge goblets. Mauve *C. speciosum* is the superior species for borders; its cultivar 'Album' the best white. Both look good in front of early-tinting shrub leaves on the woodland fringe, like the oak-leaved hydrangea, *H. quercifolia*, and the spindle *Euonymus europaeus* 'Red Cascade', which combines coloured leaves with orange and red fruits.

PONDSIDE IN AUTUMN

There is a quirky water garden, part oriental and part Scottish, at Broughton House in Kirkcudbright, made by the early twentieth-century artist E. A. Hornel. A narrow strip, it starts off in the busy High Street and finishes up in the countryside, looking across the River Dee.

I was there amid all the russets of early autumn, somewhat the worse for wear as we had been sampling malt whiskies into the early hours, but I do vividly remember the theatrical gash of a scarlet bridge – a simple painted arch – across the water, and how the colour was picked up by the spires of scarlet cups on that showy South African perennial *Schizostylis coccinea* 'Major', planted in front of the trunks of a gleaming white birch.

Schizostylis don't need to be wet, just moist, but are great finale plants for the pondside season. The sharp pink variety 'Viscountess Byng' peaks in November. Otherwise, there are leaf tints from the waterside ferns *Osmunda regalis* and *Onoclea sensibilis*, and a range of attractive seedheads, notably the moleskin sausages of the bullrushes (very invasive), which will stand proud until spring.

A CYCLAMEN CORNER

Pools of hardy pink and white cyclamen, *C. hederifolium*, are highlights of the early September garden. They look delicate but, as anyone who has tried them will know, are readily established all over the garden, including in many places – such as around tree roots, in sun and shade – where very little else will grow. As long as they get moisture, and some light, in winter and spring, they can take summer drought in their stride.

But they are no good in competition: they want their own spot, undisturbed by digging, ideally dressed with a little leafmould during a moist spell in early summer, where they can seed themselves about. It is also easy as pie to raise

thousands of seedlings yourself: look out for the ripening seedpods in summer, sow the seeds on top of a deep pot of compost, topdress with fine grit, cover with mesh against mice, put in a part-shady corner, forget about them for a couple of years, and plant out the next spring.

WOODLAND SHADE

The tall white bottlebrushes of the bugbanes, *Actaea* (formerly *Cimicifuga*), stand out well in shady autumn borders, and are a fine contrast to the tinting leaves. Although 4ft/1.25m or more, the ferny foliage and slim flowerheads fit happily at the front of the border, among hostas and hellebores. Some of them smell disgusting, others like honey or bubblegum, and among the latter I would single out green-leaved *A. matsumurae* 'Elstead' and purple-leaved *A. simplex* 'Brunette', which requires a bit more sunlight. Both look good with fuchsias.

Happily, birds aren't much tempted by scarlet skimmia fruits, which often

↑ Dry, rooty ground at the base of a tree? *Cyclamen hederifolium* grows where many plants fear to tread.

hang on right through the winter and into the next spring, when plants are brandishing their next crop of white flowers. The rocky bank of them in the woods of Portmeirion in north-west Wales, fringed with ferns, campions and bluebells, is a great sight. They show distress on poor, dry, limy soils, but otherwise make ideal short foundation shrubs for the shady border. You need one scented male pollinator to two berrying females.

Among the 4ft/1.25m varieties, *S. japonica* 'Fragrans' is an effective pollinator and *S. j.* 'Nymans' a productive female (*S.* × *confusa* 'Kew Green', the most handsome male, is not interested in the opposite sex); among the 2ft/60cm sorts, *S. j.* 'Bowles' Dwarf Male' will serve 'Bowles' Dwarf Female' and white-berried 'Wakehurst White'.

A few herbaceous plants produce berries, too, striking scarlet and white ones in the case of baneberries, *Actaea rubra* and *A. pachypoda*, borne on 2ft/60cm stems above ferny leaves. But they are both outshone by the hefty orange-fruited clubs of *Arum italicum* 'Marmoratum', which can be enormous on a retentive soil. I cut away the fading leaves and sheaths to expose them properly, and they stand out like beacons, particularly against bright foliage, like golden creeping jenny (*Lysimachia nummularia* 'Aurea') or lettuce-green polypodium ferns.

Undoubtedly the most valuable perennials for part shade, and for the edge of sunny borders, are the Japanese anemones, which start flowering in high summer and go on for a great many weeks. I think the mauve-pinks are repulsive, but *A. hupehensis* 'Hadspen Abundance' is an extremely handsome bicolour in pale pink and deep rose. *A.* × *hybrida* 'Honorine Jobert' is a superior white. The central yellow bosses of the flowers were beautifully picked out in one scheme I saw by the golden plumes of the invasive, ligularia-like perennial *Sinacalia tangutica* (syn. *Senecio tanguticus*), isolated in a moist bed behind.

Another deserving perennial of the moment is the white-flowered, green-leaved *Hosta plantaginea* 'Grandiflora'. In countries with hot summers this develops flowers of enviable proportions, but even for us it is an eyecatchingly fresh, cool feature for late in the year. The 3ft/1m blue willow gentian,

Gentiana asclepiadea, makes a good partner for it – easily grown on any moist soil.

LEAF TINTS AMONG SHRUBS AND CLIMBERS

Autumn leaf colour is more reliable in some plants than others. My Japanese maples 'Osakazuki' and 'Aconitifolium' turn bright red whatever happens. I once saw them grown with the white plumes of pampas grass and a rug of black ophiopogon leaves; a stunning colour scheme, if a little Nazi.

On the other hand, my big-leaved Japanese vine, *Vitis coignetiae*, varies greatly in intensity from year to year, presumably in response to sunshine levels. It has now reached almost to the top of one of the copper beech trees in my garden, its launchpad into the tree being a 'Cunningham's White' rhododendron, which manages to flower when the vine leaves are still small and tan. Of course it grows equally vigorously on walls and pergolas, its jungle character particularly appropriate as a backdrop to cannas and other pot-plant exotica.

Sunlight certainly makes a difference to the performance of many autumn-tinting shrubs, so as a general rule I wouldn't put any of them in too gloomy a spot. Unfortunately for many gardeners, some of the best shrubs are lime-haters: *Fothergilla major*, *Enkianthus perulatus* and *E. campanulatus*, and deciduous azaleas.

But everyone can grow *Euonymus alatus* 'Compactus', which turns one of the most spectacular lipstick reds. At Chartwell, Kent, it shines beside scarlet, greyish-leaved *Fuchsia magellanica* 'Versicolor', picking up the tints of Virginia creeper beyond. And given space for a large shrub, *Cornus kousa* seldom disappoints in its production of strawberry-like fruits and matt red leaves.

I have already mentioned the bonfire of autumn tints and coral berries you get from *Berberis wilsoniae*, and the hips on rose species. And if birds don't strip them, heavily laden cotoneasters and pyracanthas can also add a great

→ With its predatory tendrils, huge leaves, and fiery tints, *Vitis coignetiae* earns its keep spring to autumn. It needs support on walls but will make its own way up trees – and how.

deal to the autumn bonfire around gravel garden and terrace. *Cotoneaster* 'Cornubia' is particularly well-endowed, and its dark evergreen leaves, borne on tall arching branches, contrast well with the turning foliage all around them. *C. lacteus* and the greyish-leaved *C. franchetii* are favourite backdrop shrubs on the 'steppe' garden at Lady Farm.

At ground level, hostas turn buttery shades, and sited next to the still green, spotted leaves of pulmonarias, and showered upon by maple leaves, they make a fine picture. The lemon witch-hazel, *Hamamelis × intermedia* 'Pallida', turns the same colour as hostas and is a good echo ('Diane' turns orange and red).

But as the leaves fall, there is plenty of serendipity. One of the jolliest examples I have seen – fortunately not in my garden – was scarlet cherry leaves nestling around the warm orange-brown fruiting bodies of honey fungus. This is a terrible serial killer of woody plants, but it doesn't do any good removing the toadstool clumps, so you may as well enjoy them. Researchers are currently working on biological and chemical controls for this pest, but in the meantime my advice is to remove the victim tree or shrub, together with all traces of infected roots, and replant with a resistant species; information is available from the Forestry Commission (Alice Holt Lodge, Wrecclesham, Farnham, Surrey GU10 4LH), and the Royal Horticultural Society at Wisley, Surrey.

OTHER EXCELLENT AUTUMN-PERFORMING PLANTS

gravel and terrace	meadow borders	woodland glades
SHRUBS		
• *Arbutus × andrachnoides*	*Viburnum opulus*	*Callicarpa bodinieri*
• *Arbutus unedo* f. *rubra*	'Compactum'	'Profusion'
• *Ceanothus* 'Autumnal Blue'	*Viburnum opulus* 'Xanthocarpum'	*Clethra alnifolia* 'Paniculata'

↑ *Callicarpa bodinieri* 'Profusion' has berries of a unique colour. You need at least two plants for cross-pollination.

gravel and terrace	meadow borders	woodland glades
SHRUBS *cont.*		
• *Choisya ternata*	◇ *Viburnum sargentii*	◇ *Euonymus sachalinensis*
Clerodendrum	'Onondaga'	• *Fatsia japonica*
trichotomum var. *fargesii*		◇ *Heptacodium miconioides*
• *Cotoneaster conspicuus*		◇ *Hydrangea paniculata*
'Decorus'		'Grandiflora'
• *Cotoneaster microphyllus*		• *Osmanthus heterophyllus*
• *Cotoneaster salicifolius*		
'Rothschildianus'		
• *Elaeagnus* × *ebbingei*		
◇ *Hippophae rhamnoides*		
SHRUBS & CLIMBERS		
for warm walls		*for shady walls*
◇ *Clematis rehderiana*		• *Camellia sasanqua*
◇ *Hibiscus syriacus* hybrids		'Narumigata'
◇ *Vitis* 'Brant'		◇ *Fallopia baldschuanica*
◇ *Vitis vinifera* 'Purpurea'		(vigorous)
		• *Mahonia lomariifolia*
		◇ *Parthenocissus*
		tricuspidata (vigorous)
		• *Pyracantha rogersiana*
		• *Pyracantha rogersiana*
		'Flava'
		• *Pyracantha* 'Watereri'
PERENNIALS		
Aster turbinellus	*Chrysanthemum* 'Emperor of	*Aconitum carmichaelii*
Boltonia asteroides	China'	'Kelmscott'
Ceratostigma	*Physostegia virginiana*	*Kirengeshoma palmata*
plumbaginoides	'Summer Snow'	*Lobelia siphilitica*
Crocus banaticus	*Physostegia virginiana* 'Vivid'	*Saxifraga fortunei* cultivars
Crocus nudiflorus		
Eucomis bicolor		
Kniphofia thomsonii		

12 — ONWARD AND UPWARD

'Two more plants, and that's the front garden finished,' I overheard someone saying at a garden centre. But, in reality, the adventure continues – and that's what keeps you hooked. You discover that certain plants do well for you, and other plants don't. Trees and shrubs rise up, changing the habitats around them. You get new enthusiasms.

It is vital to keep a critical eye, and to scrutinize your plot continually. I remember, at the end of the season, visiting the borders of Powis Castle under Jimmy Hancock's reign as head gardener. Dreamier associations of shrubs, climbers and perennials were not to be found anywhere in Britain. And yet dotted through the beds were little canes with notes attached, indicating plants which he thought should be increased, moved, reduced or replaced. Next year, he knew he could do better.

I find that wandering around the garden with a camera concentrates the mind. Why don't I want to take a shot of this scene? If I can improve it there and then, I do. Perhaps it needs a theatrical flourish. Perhaps it just needs a bit of pruning and filleting. Perhaps a plant has to come out altogether. In Holland, gardeners think nothing of murdering trees and shrubs the minute they outgrow their position. As a result, gardens rarely develop much character. But here we are at the opposite extreme, sentimentally procrastinating even when a plant is clearly no longer earning its keep. I have been dithering over a faithful, but now decrepit, old cistus for three years.

At The Garden House, Keith Wiley often cleverly rejuvenates a scene by shaving off the lower branches of a shrub, to leave exposed trunks, and thinning its canopy at the same time. What was a thicket suddenly becomes a sculpture,

← Previous page: The spirit of high-summer meadows is captured by Tom Stuart-Smith in his borders. Here, *Echinacea purpurea* blooms among phlox, salvia, nepeta and verbascum.

with enough light for new bulb and perennial plantings around it. The practice isn't always a success. I tried it at home on a ceanothus, but it looks a bit embarrassed, like someone caught with their trousers down.

Planting things too close is a common fault, and ten years on you can find yourself with very painful decisions. The intelligent policy is to space long-term, slow-developing trees and shrubs widely, allowing for a mature spread, and to infill with fast, expendable plants, like lavatera, buddleia, ceanothus, abutilon, broom, as well as tall perennials, which can be gradually removed.

The exposure to a constant flow of ideas on design and planting keeps things lively, too. Many of these you will want to incorporate into the garden. All gardeners feed off what they see in other people's gardens, and in the wild. But slavish copying is dull. You need to give each idea your own twist.

And finally, there are all those plants that catch your eye from one year to the next, and that you itch to try out. I find it impossible to pass a good nursery without stopping for a little trawl. And then there is the challenge of finding gaps for them back home. As I overheard another gardener confiding to her friend, 'Isn't it lucky that plants die on us occasionally?'

A RECOMMENDED
LIBRARY

PLANT REFERENCE

Anthony Archer-Wills, *The Water Gardener* (Frances Lincoln, 1993).

Beth Chatto, *Beth Chatto's Gravel Garden* (Frances Lincoln, 2000).

Richard Hansen and Friedrich Stahl, *Perennials and Their Garden Habitats* (Cambridge University Press, 1993).

Alan Mitchell and Allen Coombes, *The Garden Tree* (Seven Dials, 1999).

Roger Phillips and Martyn Rix, The Pan Garden Plants Series: *Bulbs* (1989), *Conservatory and Indoor Plants* (1998), *Perennials* (1991–3), *Roses* (1988), *Shrubs* (1989).

Graham Stuart Thomas, *Ornamental Shrubs, Climbers and Bamboos* (John Murray, 1992).

—— *Perennial Garden Plants* (Dent, 1976; revised edn 1993).

PRACTICAL REFERENCE

Christopher Brickell, *Royal Horticultural Society Encyclopaedia of Gardening* (Dorling Kindersley, 1992).

George E. Brown, *The Pruning of Trees, Shrubs and Conifers* (Timber Press, 1995).

← The flowerheads of *Miscanthus sinensis* 'Rotsilber', produced in early autumn, ripen to shades of parchment and cobwebby white for the winter months.

DESIGN REFERENCE

John Brookes, *John Brookes' Garden Design Book* (Dorling Kindersley, 1991).

Terence Conran and Dan Pearson, *The Essential Garden Book* (Conran Octopus, 1998).

BEDTIME READING

Helen Dillon, *Helen Dillon on Gardening* (Town House, Dublin, 1998).

Lucy Gent, *Great Planting* (Ward Lock, 1995).

Penelope Hobhouse, *Penelope Hobhouse on Gardening* (Frances Lincoln, 1994).

Andrew Lawson, *The Gardener's Book of Colour* (Frances Lincoln, 1996).

Christopher Lloyd, *The Well-Tempered Garden* (Faber, 1970; revised edn Cassell, 2001).

—— *Christopher Lloyd's Gardening Year* (Frances Lincoln, 1999).

Piet Oudolf and Noel Kingsbury, *Designing with Plants* (Conran Octopus, 1999).

Rosemary Verey, *Good Planting* (Frances Lincoln, 1990).

ACKNOWLEDGEMENTS

There is a small band of real artists among garden photographers, and it has
been a luxury not only having Stephen Robson on the project for a full year,
but also to be able to turn to Vivien Russell, Andrew Lawson and Jerry and
Marcus Harpur to plug the gaps. Five principal gardens are featured, in
addition to my own, and I am very grateful to their owners and makers for
allowing repeated visits: Keith Wiley and the Trustees of The Garden House,
Buckland Monachorum, Devon; Judy and Malcolm Pearce, Lady Farm,
Chelwood, Somerset; Fiona and Desmond Heyward, Haseley Court, Oxford;
Tom Stuart-Smith, The Barn, Serge Hill, Abbot's Langley, Hertfordshire; and
Gareth Hughes, 31 Queen's Road, Sheen, London. (Note that only The Garden
House and Lady Farm are regularly open to the public.)

I have been lucky to have had encouragement and feedback from an
excellent literary agent, Anthony Goff, and publisher, Tom Weldon, throughout the writing. In fact – somewhat unusually – this project has been a pleasure
from start to finish. Many thanks to John Hamilton and Nicky Barneby for
taking such care over the design of the book, and to Sarah Day for her editorial
management; to Annie Lee for her meticulous editing; to Tony Lord for
scrutinizing the text for any errors in plant names, which taxonomists change
the moment you have learned them; and to Ian Smith, without whom my
garden would be permanent jungle.

Page numbers in **bold** type refer to illustrations.